ANGELA PREUSS
Wizard of Party-Plan S

MW00444624   ique,

Life is full of opportunities, every problem can be a challenge to rise to greater heights of personal achievement. Angela Preuss has seen life that way, and she found a way through the challenges of life to success and happiness as wife, mother, and business executive.

Three prospectives have shaped her life: (1) religious faith, (2) firm belief that family and business career can be wedded in a woman's life, and (3) robust determination that "I was born poor, but I will NOT die poor."

From her childhood as a daughter of immigrant parents in the "Little Italy" community in lower Manhattan, Angela rose to the achievement of TEN MIL-LION DOLLARS in annual sales for her division of a major party-plan company.

Read in this story of her life a true "Horatio Alger" example of success and achievement. Learn how a young girl with only high school education succeeded in becoming a successful business executive. Learn the keys she discovered for using party-plan sales to reach her goal of financial success. Discover for yourself how enthusiastic self-confidence and sound business principles can enable you to succeed. In these pages meet Angela Preuss and learn the secrets of her superstar achievements.

Says of Angela Preuss...

In Coppercraft Guild she participated in developing management philosophy and sales programs, selling one product and using one system of selling. As field president of Passeport Boutique, she is developing a unique system of organization and marketing.

The key to success for a company in party-plan is sales leadership and organization in the style and character of Angela Preuss's operation. Her approach is people oriented, success motivated, and profit producing. Her program of training and motivation takes people without special skills and develops them into effective and prosperous business people.

Angela Preuss

WIZARD OF PARTY-PLAN SALES

The Success Story
of a
TEN MILLION DOLLAR Sales Wizard
by
Sherrill Stevens

Contents

Preface

Why would a book be written about me? Sales has been my area of activity and expertise, but something about the way I succeeded at it made people want to learn more. In my business and personal contacts I was often asked questions which indicated that the askers were interested in what makes me tick.

Marlene White was the very first person to suggest that I write a book about myself and my success. She was inspired by my achievements and wanted me to share some of my secrets. Barbara Grogan, a friend who practiced "reading sticks," said to me that every time she "read my sticks" they would say, "You'll write a book." But I discounted their suggestions, for sales and not writing was my thing.

Then on February 23, 1976 my cousin Jo Nachman gave me a "Nothing Book," a book of blank pages, with the suggestion that it was time for me to write my story. My mind toyed with the idea but I did nothing more until December, 1979. Phyllis Scruggs telephoned from Richmond, Virginia and asked, "Would you be interested in publishing a book about yourself?"

Phyllis introduced me to Dr. Fred Skaggs and the people of Skipworth Press, a Richmond based publishing company which specializes in religious, inspirational, and success-oriented books. That inquiry and introduction set the gears into motion at a time which seems genuinely providential, for Dr. Skaggs called for an interview appointment just two weeks before my position with Coppercraft Guild was terminated.

Before the scheduled interview took place I was fired, and consequently the work on this book was begun at a time of severe personal trauma. My brief time of unemployment did make it possible for me to devote time to furnishing the material for the book however. I furnished the materials by taped interview for the author who is general editor of Skipworth Press.

My purpose in sharing this story is twofold. I hope by telling of my achievements in party-plan sales to enhance the image of the industry itself. And I hope by telling how I managed my roles in marriage, family, and career that many wives and mothers who need or choose to be employed will be encouraged that the roles can be related successfully.

I dedicate this book about myself to my mother, Mrs. Grace Parisi, and to my husband Carl. I express appreciation to those who have encouraged me to tell this story in print and to the publishers who worked with me to bring it into publication.

ANGELA PREUSS
Patchogue, NY 11772

Introduction

ANGELA PREUSS
Wizard of Party-Plan Sales

Angela was eleven. It was the spring of 1942. The fifth grade at PS 248 was casting for a class play "Janie Travels Abroad." The play was a story about a little girl going from country to country. Janie's part was to introduce each scene with a narration of something distinctive about the country being visited in that scene. Then players from the class would act out a presentation about that country. Angela wanted so very much to be chosen to play the part of Janie, but Angela Parisi was a little Italian girl. Every time the teacher asked who else would like to "try-out" for Janie, Angela eagerly raised her hand. But every time her hand was ignored, and Angela was passed over in favor of one of the "Americanized" girls in the Brooklyn school.

The casting went on until every part in the play had been assigned, and Angela had not been given a chance to even try-out for any part at all. She went home that day crushed inside, feeling harshly discriminated against, and sure in her heart that it was because she was from an Italian immigrant family.

Play rehearsals got started and soon it was obvious that the girl who had been chosen to play the part of Janie just couldn't do it. Another had to be chosen. Angela raised her hand again, almost jumping out of her seat as she said, "I can do it! I can do it!" Two of the teachers got together, talked it over for a few minutes, and finally decided to take a chance and let her have a try at it. Angela was given the part; she learned all her lines easily; rehearsals were soon finished; and the play turned out to be a hit.

After the play turned out to be so popular with the students and teachers at school, it was decided to have it presented for the parents and adults of the community at the spring Parent-Teacher Association night. On the same evening, as part of the same program, a flower show was scheduled and children were asked to bring flowers from home to be entered in the show. Angela's mother had a beautiful begonia which Angela wanted to enter, but she was afraid her mother would never agree. The flower was in a beautiful but heavy jardiniere and Angela's mother thought she could never carry it to the school without dropping it. But Angela kept begging and finally persuaded her mother to let her take the begonia and enter it in the flower show.

On the night of the PTA meeting Angela had one of the proudest experiences of her life. The play was a hit with the parents, just as it had been with the students at school, and Angela was the center of the applause. In addition her mother's begonia won first place in the flower show. When Mrs. Parisi was called to the stage to receive the award for her flower, her words to the audience in her distinctive Italian accent were, "I'a is'a *Janie's* mutha." Mrs. Parisi was far prouder of her daughter than she was of her begonia. Angela went home that night beaming inside with the joy of having pleased her mother, who along with her husband Carl have been the two most important and influential people in the life of Angela Parisi Preuss.

Chapter I

Angela Preuss: Her Roots

Angela Preuss's mother Graziella (Grace) Di Terlizzi was born in Bisciglie, a small town on the Adriatic coast of Italy. She married Felice Petruno of Biscelge, Italy, and following World War I it became possible for Felice and Grace to emigrate to America. He received his passage free as a veteran's benefit. They traveled by steerage on a trip which took twenty-one days at sea. Grace was pregnant at the time and the voyage was an almost intolerable experience for her.

The Petruno Family in America

Coming to America represented a new beginning in a land of opportunity for the Petrunoes. They arrived in New York City and settled in the "Little Italy" section of lower Manhattan. Soon thereafter a daughter Josephine (Josie) was born. Those were difficult days for the family, for Felice could not find work and he was deeply shamed at not being able to provide for his family. Grace did find work in one of the ladies' garment "sweat factories" where she earned from $12 to $20 per week. Her earnings were adequate to provide necessities for them while Felice walked the streets day after day looking for work.

After a whole year of looking and waiting, Felice finally found a job as a construction worker. He was so thrilled. Things looked good for the family at last in their new home in America. Then tragedy struck. Just three days after Felice went to work on his new job, Grace came home in the afternoon from her job at the factory to find a crowd of people gathered at her home. They told her the sad news that Felice had been killed in an accident at work. Grace Petruno was left a young widow with a little child in this new land far away from her remaining family. She was a person of sturdy character, however, so she set about to support herself and her daughter in spite of the strange newness of the country and the language barrier which existed for her as a recent immigrant.

The Years of Widowhood

Grace moved herself and Josie to a third floor apartment at 197 Hester Street in lower New York-Manhattan. That was to be home to them for the next thirteen years. There Angela was born and lived the first years of her life. People and experiences which influenced her infancy and childhood touched her life there.

On the third floor at 197 Hester Street there were four apartments. In one of those three-room apartments lived the Volpe family, "Grandma" Volpe and her nine children. She was widowed so everyone had to work to support their family. One daughter, Mary, was semi-invalid, having been crippled by infantile paralysis (polio) the same year that Franklin Delano Roosevelt was stricken. Mary was able to care for Josie while Grace worked in the factory sewing beaded handbags day after day.

These two widowed women who worked to support their families lived a very frugal life. They worked long, hard hours just to provide basic necessities. Grace Petruno would go to the factory and sew handbags all day. Then after work she would sew on men's coats at home until dark. The families went to bed at dark to save money because it took a quarter-dollar in the meter to operate the gas lamps in their apartments. She would then arise at break of dawn and sew on the coats again until it was time to go to her daytime job at the factory. So her life in those days was one of hard work and ambition. Being an immigrant and not a citizen, no welfare assistance of any kind was available to her. But she did not complain, for she believed this country to be a land of opportunity. A conviction which she often expressed to her family was, "I'd rather be dead in America than alive in Europe, because here you can work and make something of yourself."

Domenico Parisi then came on the scene. He too was born in Biscelge, Italy. He was one of ten children in a poor family, so he had to go to work early in life to help earn a living for his family. Domenico was a scholarly boy who caught the attention of the brothers in the Catholic school. They wanted to train him for the priesthood but his family would not consent, because they needed what he could earn to help support the family. The brothers did teach him to write in an ornate scroll like the biblical style, a characteristic he continued throughout his life.

Being of a poor family, there was no money to buy Domenico a passage to America when he decided that he wanted to go to that new country to settle. He was convinced that better opportunities awaited him there, however, so he joined the merchant marine and then "jumped ship" as soon as they arrived in New York.

This young Italian immigrant was an enterprising fellow. He set himself up in the rag business with only a cart. With his cart he picked up scrap rag cuttings in the garment factories, along with waste paper, baled the scrap and waste and sold it in New Jersey for recycling. He got paid twice, once for taking away the waste from the factories and again for the bales of waste material he sold. From the beginning he was an independent businessman who made money to provide for his family by his own initiative and energy.

But the rag business was not a clean business, and Domenico was always dirty when he was on the job. So when he noticed the young widow, Grace Petruno, and was attracted to her, she wanted no part of him. Domenico fell more and more under her spell, while Grace kept a cool distance. He realized that she was offended by his dirty appearance, so after work he cleaned up and went to court her properly.

Now Domenico was a romantic at heart. His way of courting Grace was to sit on the landing at 197 Hester Street and read poetry to her, or play his guitar and sing in his native Italian, "My love, do you hear me?"

After a period of courtship they married and he adopted Josie. These were to become the parents of Angela Parisi Preuss; he an industrious businessman, and she a wise and worthy woman who became the pillar of the family and the home. Grace Parisi had only a third grade education, but she knew what really counts in life. She built love and hospitality into the very fabric of their family life, so while the family was poor in things, they were rich in the things that matter.

The Parisi Family

Domenico Parisi stopped Grace from working in the factory. He had vowed that she would never again work outside their home after she became his wife. She was to be wife and mother, and the importance of that role in her parental family surely influenced the value Angela later placed on that role for herself in her family.

Five children were to be born to Domenico and Grace Parisi. The first was a son who was stillborn. The loss of their first child was a deep and traumatic blow to them, a sadness over which they both grieved for a long, long time.

The second Parisi child was a girl named Rosie. At six months of age she became very ill when stricken by infantile paralysis and was left a deaf mute. Her handicap became a matter of involvement for the entire family. In many ways the life of the family members revolved around being in the right place at the right time to meet Rosie's needs. During the infant and early childhood years she was almost inseparable from her mother.

New York law required that at age five she be placed in a special boarding school, the Lexington School for the Deaf. When time came for Rosie to go away to school, her nearly inseparable tie with her mother had to be broken, and it was an experience of agony for both of them. She had to be literally pulled away from her mother as she clung in fear to her. That, of course, really tore at Grace's heart. Mrs. Parisi walked around the school building for hours, listening to Rosie inside screaming, before she could bring herself to go away home and leave her little daughter there.

When Mrs. Parisi learned she was going to have another child, she was quite concerned because neither of her two previous children was healthy. She went to a physician who gave her a series of six injections to help prevent any defect in her unborn child. In her seventh month, when she received the sixth injection, she suffered a severe reaction. She swelled badly, lost her hair and nails, and the physicians thought she could live no more than two or three hours. A priest was called to give her the last rites of her church.

Mr. Parisi arrived at the hospital about that time, saw the priest, and went into a violent rage. He drove the priest away and refused to let him administer the rites. He insisted, "My wife is not going to die!" Grace did pull through the crisis and days later returned home to recover. Her recovery was slow for she had to learn to walk again and it took long weeks before her hair and nails were grown out again. During that time she was so very embarrassed at her appearance, and all the time she lived in fear that her baby would be affected, but she was not.

That baby was Angela. She was born at home, at 197 Hester

Street, on September 25, 1931. She was a healthy and beautiful baby. She was born with blue eyes, and that was quite unusual for a child of an Italian family. Her friends rejoiced with Grace and Domenico, and told them that if Angela had been born at a hospital instead of at home they would surely have believed they switched babies with someone to get a healthy, blue-eyed child. Because of her mother's health problems, Angela's birth cost them a thousand dollars. That was such a lot of money in the days of the Great Depression that Angela's parents called her their "Million Dollar Baby."

The next child born in the Parisi family was another girl whom they named Betty. She was born the same day the Dionne Quintuplets were born in Canada. Domenico had been hoping very much for a boy that time, so he said to his wife, "Grace, if you had to give me another girl, why do you drag this out? The Canadian woman gave her husband five girls at one time."

Betty was a beautiful child with curly hair and a great, outgoing personality. She was a joy to her family, and often the envy of Angela as they grew up but a close and dear sister who has shared so much of life with her.

Then, at last, came a son to the Parisies. At his birth Domenico was simply beside himself with joy. Over and over he said, "My son, my son — just look at him Grace, look at those big black eyes." Mario was the last child in the family, and as with every family each child was unique and distinctive, and each one influenced every other one as they grew up together.

Angela's Childhood

In her infancy Angela was influenced by neighbors as well as by family. The Volpes, who were neighbors at their Hester Street home, were very important influences in her life. Mary Volpe was babysitter for all the Parisi children. One of Angela's childhood memories is of Mary singing nursery rhymes to her brother Mario when he was a baby. Mary and her sister Catherine (Katie) neither ever married, so they kept a close relationship with the Parisi family through the years. Katie was godmother to Angela, and she was like a fairy godmother too. Having no children of her own, Katie showered affection on Angela and did many things for her through the years to make her feel special.

When Angela was four years old, the Parisi family moved from

Manhattan to Brooklyn, and that was like moving from downtown to suburbia. All through the years the family was bound together by a strong family love and they did lots of family things together. One of their favorite outings was a day at the beach. Grace would take the children to Coney Island by subway to spend a day. Mary Volpe would go along with them to help care for the children. Angela's chore was to carry the beach umbrella which was to be shade for Mario. Those were wholesome days, filled with good and happy experiences: swimming in the ocean, building sandcastles, and just lying in the sun.

During those years Rosie was at boarding school. She came home on weekends and during the summer. Her handicap had a great influence on Angela. Many times when Angela was a child she heard her mother tell over and over again about the heart-breaking experience of having Rosie pulled from her arms when she had to leave her at the special school for deaf children. Hearing that story of agony and separation made a lasting impression on Angela and helped her become very sensitive to the feelings of people, especially those who are having difficult times in life.

A weekly ritual developed in the Parisi family for getting Rosie back and forth to school. Because she was deaf mute, they arranged for someone to always go with her. At first their father would go for her on Friday and take her back on Sunday afternoon. Later it became Josie's task, and after Angela was twelve that ritual became her family chore. Until Rosie graduated Angela went back and forth with her on the subway between home and school each week.

During those years Angela became involved with the school, and her exposure to the handicapped children there increased her sensitivity to the needs and feelings of people. One of the memorable experiences of Angela's youth was Rosie's graduation from the Lexington School. On that occasion Angela's mother pointed out to her the famed Hellen Keller and her teacher Annie who were present. During those years Angela seriously considered making a career of working with deaf persons. Rosie had a very special place in Angela's life, and it seemed to her that she had been given the voice which Rosie did not have.

Betty was also a very special person to Angela. Betty was pretty and talented. Her parents sent her to dancing school where she learned to dance on her toes. That often made her the center of attention as she performed her ballet routines. Angela, by contrast, was quite sensitive about her straight hair and skinny frame. She was quiet, studious, and sensitive to people; and though she did not feel jealous of Betty, she did feel overshadowed by her outgoing younger sister.

As she grew up Angela was very concious, probably too much so, of the fact that she was an "immigrant child." That feeling was more her own than caused by things others said or did, though there were incidents like the one about being passed by so long in the try-outs for the part of Janie in the fifth grade play.

What was it that made a little Italian girl growing up in Brooklyn in the nineteen thirties feel different and discriminated against? Angela was sensitive to both looks and manners. She was Italian growing up among other children of Jewish and English background. Her family language had the distinctive Italian quality about it. Her mother's choice of clothes was Italian in taste. Her parents had not been schooled in the niceties of etiquette, and they had had no opportunities to learn from exposure, so they could not teach these to their children in the home. Angela was aware in her childhood that at their house the table was not "set" properly the way it was at friends' houses when she went to visit. At her house the utensils were just put on the table any which way. At school she was exposed to children who had some cultural upbringing, and Angela sensed that this was lacking in her home. She wanted so very much to learn "nicer" ways, and be more refined like some of the other girls, but she didn't know who to learn from.

At school the "teachers' pets" were always the Americanized children, or that's how it seemed to Angela. They were the ones who got to erase the chalkboards and do other little special favors for the teachers. Angela was sure the discrimination was because she was Italian. She didn't like for her mother to come to school, because her dress and speech were so distinctively Italian it called attention to their immigrant background. Angela would feel a tinge of shame about her Italian family, and then she would feel guilty because she really loved her mother and would have been crushed if her mother had known how she felt. The experience of being different from her peers was really creating problems of strong personal feeling for Angela as she grew up.

While the family did not have a cultural heritage, Mr. Parisi loved art, opera, music, and poetry. He read classics such as the works of Shakespeare and Dante. He insisted that his children receive artistic training, mainly music. Betty was given dancing and piano lessons; Mario was taught the accordion; and the violin was chosen for Angela. Domenico himself took piano lessons after he was middle-aged. Angela remembered the strange experience of their father having to ask his children, "Which is the *A* note?" Between themselves they chuckled at the idea of a "grown man" struggling to learn to play "Jingle Bells."

Such was the childhood of Angela Parisi. There were good experiences of warm and loving family life. There was the frustrating contrast between love of art and lack of culture. There was pride in achievement and lack of pride in her heritage because she was of immigrant Italian stock. Through it all she was being conditioned to determine that she would prove to the world that she was the equal of her peers in ability and achievement.

The Years of Her Youth

By junior high years Angela had come to love being the center of attention. To get that attention she often disturbed her classes at school by clowning around. That went on until she got into trouble for it. Mr. Schwartz, her history teacher, asked for her mother to come to the school for a conference. Mr. Schwartz reported to Mrs. Parisi that Angela was bright, but that she was not studying, and she was disturbing the class by cutting up. Mrs. Parisi asked, "Where is Angela sitting?" "In the back of the room," Mr. Schwartz answered. "Put her up front, right before you," Mrs. Parisi said, "and she won't trouble you anymore." So the conference ended, but that wasn't the end of the matter.

When Mrs. Parisi got home with Angela, she grabbed her by the collar, shook her good, and said, "I'm so ashamed of you. Understand this, if I'm ever called to the school again, I won't even go. Maybe you should be back in kindergarten if you're going to act like a child." Angela was shocked when she realized how deeply her mother had been humiliated by what had happened. It was a great lesson for her, for by it she became aware that by her actions she could hurt others as well as herself. Being a sensitive person, and not wanting to hurt her mother, Angela caused no more trouble at school. She made her way through the remainder of her school years with flying colors.

Angela was growing up, and as a teenager she discovered that she wanted to go out and do things with other teenage friends. But her mother was very strict. When Angela would ask *if* she might go out with friends, her mother would almost always say "No." So Angela learned to use a positive approach. Instead of asking if she might do something, Angela would make a statement assuming that she could do it. She would say, "After school I'm going over to the soda shop with friends," or "Friday night I'm going to sleep over at June's house." She learned that it worked, and she didn't forget it. Making a positive approach became a primary technique she used for getting results later in her selling career.

Lessons were learned from other experiences which were not so pleasant or positive. Angela disliked her violin lessons, and she especially hated the finger exercises which are so necessary for learning to play the violin. But her father kept on insisting that she continue her lessons. Every Tuesday and Friday her teacher, Mr. Bartinelli, would come to the house for her lessons. Over and over the finger exercises had to be practiced and played. The music book Mr. Bartinelli used for lessons had several pages of those hated finger exercises. One day Angela ripped out those pages from the teacher's book, tore them to bits, took them down to the corner of the street, and threw them down the storm sewer. She thought that if only she could get rid of those pages, maybe Mr. Bartinelli would not notice and she could get by without those finger exercises.

On the day of her next violin lesson, however, just as you would guess, Mr. Bartinelli asked, "Where are the finger exercise pages?" Angela pretended not to know, laughing inside at the idea that she'd never have to do them again. It didn't turn out that way though, for on the day of her next lesson he brought a new book which had even more of the exercises than the old one had had. Angela learned that such devious schemes don't often work.

As soon as she could get by with it, Angela gave up the violin and got away from music lessons. She was interested in teenage group activities, and Frank Sinatra was the teenagers' idol of the day. Once Angela cut classes at school to go with some friends to see and hear Sinatra at the Paramount Theater. Instead of getting home at the regular time to arrive from school, it was six o'clock before she got home. When her father learned what she had done, he was horrified that she would cut class to go see that "skinny, blue-eyed singer." Again, Angela had disappointed one of her parents, and she was ashamed for having hurt her father, for parental approval was very important to her.

In 1947, when Angela was in high school, her father bought a farm on Long Island. They had moved from the inner city to the suburbs, and now they moved to the country. He thought it was going to be great for the family to raise their own chickens and pigs, and keep their own cow for milk and butter. Angela hated living on the farm. She didn't like feeding chickens and pigs, and they lived eleven miles from school, which meant she had to ride a school bus and could not stay for any after-school activities. There was one good thing about living on the Long Island farm, however. There she met her husband-to-be, Carl Preuss, who lived on another farm just down the road.

Angela didn't like to work on the family farm, but she learned quickly to like to do work when she could earn money for doing it. At age fourteen she got her first job to earn money. It was a job picking up potatoes. At five o'clock in the morning a truck would pick up workers in the community and take them to the potato fields where they would work all day filling baskets with potatoes at seven cents per bushel. Angela learned quickly that if you picked-up potatoes fast you could fill more baskets and make more money. She became an expert both at picking-up potatoes and at counting by sevens to add up her earnings. Even at that early age Angela was motivated by a feeling of satisfaction at being able to generate increased earnings by her own efforts. That motivation was later shaped into something of a philosophy of life by her. Many times she said, "I was born poor, but I will not die poor." That determination gave her a great drive to work hard for financial success.

But she had some hard lessons to learn about how to succeed in the business world. When Angela was sixteen, she was eligible to get her "working papers," so she got a job in the village of Patchogue working at the ice cream parlor. Her first assignment was to make ice cream balls, ice cream cones, and fill orders behind the counter. She thought, "If I give big cones and sprinkle them with nuts, everybody will want to buy from us and our business will boom because we'll be known for giving big servings for the money. But the boss didn't agree with the way she was working. He kept telling her she was making the cones too big, but she kept on making them just as large as before. She was strong-headed and wanted to show the boss that she really knew how to make his business go. So then on Friday he said to her, "I can't use you anymore. I tried to tell you how to make the cones, but you just wouldn't listen so I'll have to dismiss you." Angela was fired, and she went home crushed. She just couldn't understand, for she had been excited about being such a great worker on her job. Her image of herself was one of a fast worker who made great ice cream cones. She just couldn't understand the rejection.

At home she told her mother that she had been fired, and Mrs. Parisi asked why. Angela said, "I don't know," but she did tell her mother about the hassle they had had over the size of the cones she made. Then her wise mother said, "Angela, you must learn that when you work for someone who pays you, you don't make ice cream balls the size *you want to,* you make them the size *he tells you to.*" So Angela went to the owner of the ice cream parlor the next day and begged for her job back. She told him she realized she had been wrong and that she would make the cones the way he told her to. She got her job back and she learned a valuable lesson, for she learned to follow instructions carefully. That lesson was important to her later, first as a sales counselor and then as a managing supervisor.

One day Bonnie, the girl who waited tables at the ice cream parlor didn't come in, so the boss asked Angela if she would like to leave behind the counter and wait tables that day. That was her first experience away from behind the fountain. When she went to clear one of the tables, she found a dime lying on it. She asked the boss what she should do with it, and he said, "That's for you. It's a tip." Angela, not knowing what a tip was, asked what it meant. The boss explained that it was extra payment for giving good service. Angela's reaction was, "For Me?!" A big smile came over her face. She had learned a new word that day, and she had also learned another way to make additional money. Making money by hard work and good service was becoming a way of life for her.

Angela Parisi: Young Adult

Academic courses in high school didn't provide her training in any job skills, so job hunting wasn't easy for Angela after high school graduation. She decided she wasn't interested in college, for Carl had come into her life and marriage was what she had on her mind.

Angela had dated other boys; but Carl Preuss, that handsome young man four years older than she, from the farm down the road, was the person who really warmed her heart most of all. Then came her senior class trip to Washington, D.C. just before high school graduation. Angela was away for several days with her classmates and had opportunity to go out with several of the boys, but none of them really interested her. When they returned home to Long Island, however, Carl was waiting for her in his 1932 Chevy. The sight of him made her heart turn flips. That convinced her she really loved him and wanted to marry him, so to be Carl Preuss' wife became the goal toward which she began to make all her plans.

Following high school graduation she needed a job because she wanted to have $1000 saved by the time of their wedding. Her studies in school had not equipped her with any special skills for employment, so she just had to go out and look for a job she could do or for which they would train her. Job hunting took Angela to a nearby state mental hospital. No jobs were available in the offices, but they could use her as an aide on the wards. Angela had no idea what she was getting into, and the only question she asked about the job was what it paid. The salary was $45 every two weeks. That sounded pretty good to her, and it was a steady job, so she took it.

The job was full of shocking surprises and lessons for her. During a period of on-the-job-training, she and the other trainees worked for some time on each of the different wards of the hospital. There were violent patients, "cold tub" treatments, and shock therapy, all of which were quite strange and very disturbing to a young lady who had not been exposed to those things before. Angela felt better about the job once the training was over and she had a ward assignment with a particular group of patients. But even there she had a lot to learn.

Angela's first specific patient assignment was to work with a Mrs. DeLuca, who felt very sorry for herself and so she began immediately to tell her sad story to Angela. Now Angela in her youth and inexperience had no idea what it is like to deal with a person who has a disordered mind. She tried to reason with Mrs. DeLuca and persuade her that life wasn't really so dark after all. As the conversation went on, Angela thought she was making real progress. Within an hour she was thinking that she about had Mrs. DeLuca "cured." Then her patient started the sad story all over again and it dawned on Angela that she had made no progress at all in helping her. Through that early experience Angela began to realize something of the frustration involved in working with people who have unbalanced minds.

At the mental hospital, Angela's permanent assignment was on a senile patient ward. One row of patients was her responsibility, and she took pride in conscientiously caring for them. She kept them very clean and tidy.

The supervising nurse on that ward was a Mrs. Donahue. She was really an "old biddy" with a harsh Irish brogue, who wore the stiffest starched uniform she could get, maintained a very austere air, and marched around inspecting the place like a hard-boiled Army sergeant.

The nurses in the hospital wore white uniforms and the aides wore gray ones, and Mrs. Donahue never let the aides forget the difference in rank between them. She looked down on them with a condescending attitude, and showed more concern about the shine on the floors than she did for the patients and attendants on the ward. Angela hated the lack of concern and personal respect for others, and she never forgot how it feels to be treated that way. An attitude was shaping itself inside Angela Parisi, an attitude which had been nurtured in her family heritage, and now in young adulthood it became a conviction of life for her. That attitude and conviction was that human dignity belongs to everyone, to janitors and other laborers as well as to executives and superstars.

Angela worked hard and saved her money. She had a goal, and she had the drive and determination needed to reach it. By the time her planned wedding date arrived, she had her $1000 in the bank in a savings account.

Chapter II

The Struggles of a Young Family

Carl and Angela Preuss were married on August 26, 1950 in the Roman Catholic Church in Patchogue, New York. She was eighteen and he was twenty-two. Their wedding day was a perfectly beautiful sunny day, and the wedding was a gala event. The ladies were dressed in lovely gowns and the men wore white tuxedoes. Angela was chaffeured to the church in a big, black limousine. Family, relatives, and friends gathered for the wedding, and Angela regaled in the love of her groom, the pride of her parents, and the attention of the crowd on her wedding day.

The reception was a "sit-down dinner" in a lovely banquet hall. Two hundred guests were included and a band played all through the festive evening. Then Carl and Angela went away for their honeymoon.

On returning from their honeymoon, Carl and Angela settled into a little apartment in Medford, Long Island and Angela went back to work. She continued in her job at the state mental hospital, even though she disliked working there under Mrs. Donahue's stern supervision, because she and Carl needed the money she was earning to help them get started as a family.

After they were married several months, Angela became pregnant but she kept on working. Hospital rules required pregnant employees to stop work in their sixth month, but Angela "carried small," so she kept her pregnancy secret and worked until she was in her ninth month.

All this time she continued to work on the wards. Hospital supervisors recognized her potential and offered her opportunities to train for different jobs and for advancement. Angela was not interested because she did not plan to make a career of working in a mental hospital. She turned down an opportunity to go into nursing

19

training for that reason. She turned down an opportunity to move from ward duty to the hospital switchboard because she was afraid to be alone in the big administration building during night shifts.

As the birth of her baby approached, time came when she had to leave her job at the hospital. Mrs. Donahue told her, as she was preparing to leave, that she would soon be back on her job there. Angela replied, "Never, never will I come back to work here and to work for you." Her hospital career ended when she left for the birth of her first baby.

Family and Careers Begin

Their daughter Deborah was born April 29, 1952. She immediately became the center of Carl and Angela's lives. At that time they were living in a three-room apartment. It was a little cramped for them, but it was okay for a couple with one little child. Carl was working at a railroad job and his earnings were very limited. After paying the necessary household expenses, they found that he could have only a couple of dollars each week for pocket money. Things were financially tight for them and that wasn't a comfortable feeling. There was little for Angela to do except keep the apartment in the mornings and in the afternoons dress her baby and walk her in her carriage.

On one August afternoon that year, Angela's mother-in-law was hostess for a White Cross home-party in her back yard. Gertrude Klein was the demonstrator of the White Cross home products for the party, and in addition to selling the products she also gave a recruiting talk. The home-party-plan for selling appealed to Angela. The idea that people could gather at the home of a friend and buy products they saw demonstrated there really attracted her. The opportunity to be at home with her baby during the day, and then earn income by selling at home-parties in the evenings interested her. Gertrude Klein's recruiting talk really got to her.

That night at home she told Carl she was interested in taking a job selling at home-parties. He was puzzled and asked her why. She explained that her housework in the small apartment only took a small part of her day, that she was bored and wanted to do something with the ambitious vein that ran through her, and that she also didn't like the family having to live on such limited income so she wanted to help by earning additional money. Angela persuaded Carl to agree for her to try her hand at party-plan selling.

A new career for her had begun.

The second Preuss child, a son David, was born on October 17, 1953, when Deborah was eighteen months old. Angela continued her White Cross sales work up until time for her baby to be born, and then shortly she went back to her work again. With two little babies and an apartment to care for, however, she found herself really staying busy.

Carl's job with the railroad was a dead-end job which wasn't satisfying to him; it didn't pay much; it offered no promise for advancement; and therefore, it was a job with no bright future for him. What he really wanted to do was go into business for himself. So he quit his job with the railroad and started operating a small gas station. He had only one gas pump and one outside service bay. It was a small business in a small town, but it did offer Carl an opportunity to get out of a salaried job and into business on his own.

With two children in the family, they were too crowded in the little apartment. Carl and his brother-in-law had built a small house in their off-duty time which they hoped to sell and make a profit on the side. Carl and Angela bought the other half-interest in the house from the brother-in-law and moved into it before their third child was born.

Angela was still working for White Cross and doing well by holding four home-parties each week. She was able to help provide for the family's needs while Carl was getting started in his business. But White Cross party-plan selling also involved packaging and delivering, so Angela found herself working day and night to keep up with the responsibilities of family, home, and job.

Then Donald was born on May 5, 1955, their third child in four years. It was all too much. Angela learned that she simply couldn't carry that much load. There were more things to be done than she could turn to during the hours of the passing days. She had to give up her party-plan business.

Careers Change and Develop

In the meantime Carl moved from the small gas station where he started into business to a Gulf Oil dealership. That business was a big station on a main highway with three service bays. The gasoline business has seasonal fluctuations, and during slack times Carl tended to get restless. He had ambitions to build his business and branch out into sidelines. He and Angela decided to use some money which had come as gifts on the occasion of Debbie's christening and buy a lawn mower sharpening machine. With that machine Carl began a personal business of servicing lawn mowers. He put a sign outside his station which read "Lawn Mowers Sharpened And Repaired."

The rent on Carl's station was based on gasoline sales, so in summer when sales were high the rent was good; but in winter when sales were off the rent dropped down, and the Gulf Oil people didn't like that. Neither did they like the clutter around the station which Carl's lawn mower repair work caused. Disagreements arose between them, so Carl decided to leave the Gulf gasoline station and go into the lawn mower and equipment business full-time. That change in business would cause some big changes to happen for the Preuss family in many other ways.

Carl had to have a shop for his new business. They sold the little house they had lived in for only a year and a half, and they bought a house on a corner property in the town of Patchogue nearby. It was zoned for business so they could live in the house and build a shop on the same lot. Carl's first shop was a small 20x20 foot building with a sign out front, "Carl's Lawn Mowers — Sharpened and Repaired."

Like most new businesses, it seemed to be all outgo and no income when it came to money. And for a lawn mower business, winter was a very slow time. Family finances got to be a problem again, so Angela pushed the panic button — it was time for her to go back to work in spite of the fact that they had three pre-school children.

But the White Cross Company had gone out of the home-party sales business. A new company came on the scene for Angela however, and that was a significant point in her career. Gertrude Daniels had been a White Cross supervisor, and she knew about Angela's effectiveness in party-plan sales work. She had, in the meantime, joined a new company whose product-line was home decor items. At that time the company was still a young company, only six years old, and Gertrude Daniels was busy recruiting a sales force for her unit in that company. It happened that she contacted Angela just at the time the Preuss family financial situation made it necessary for her to go to work again.

Angela was frightened at the idea of trying to sell $14.95 ice buckets instead of $.39 bottle brushes, but she felt driven to take the job anyway because of the family's need for additional income. So Angela began her career in home decor party-plan sales which was to continue very successfully for the next twenty-three years.

Carl's business began to grow and prosper, and soon Angela was earning enough money to support the family, so they were able to turn Carl's company profits into expansion capital for increasing the company operation. But two thriving businesses in one family began to bring pressures on family schedules, especially during the busy seasons. That situation led to the installation of an intercom system between the house and the shop so Carl could monitor the children as they slept in the evenings while he worked on repairs in the shop and Angela was away doing her home shows.

All through those years of rearing their family and building their businesses, Carl and Angela operated without using baby sitters. Friday nights were the most difficult times because the store was open and there were customers to serve. Carl simply could not attend to needs in the house while he was operating the store and waiting on customers on those open store nights. The flexibility of party-plan selling permitted Angela to solve that problem by not booking any shows on Friday nights. Those years when the children were small, and Carl and Angela were working so hard developing their young businesses, were very close and happy years for the Preuss family.

Prosperity and Problems

One of the dangers which arose for them during those years was Angela's love for her work. She became so engrossed in it that she developed a pattern of working seven days a week. Carl operated his business only six days, so Angela looked to him to care for the children on Sundays to free her for uninterrupted business work at her desk. Resentment began to develop with Carl because of it. Angela was making time for her work and for others who were business associates, but she had begun unconsciously to neglect her family and her husband. One day Carl said to her, "You love your business more than you love me." "Why do you say that?" she asked him, and he replied, "Because you spend more time with it." With those words Angela became aware that she was indeed becoming addicted to her work. She did some self-examination and found that she was beginning to love her work more than being wife, mother, and family member. So she began to discipline herself to break that addiction and reorient her life. She loved her husband and children, and did not want anything to come between them, however subtly and unconsciously it might happen. Since her desk was in the house, she developed a habit of covering it with a sheet on Sundays to remind her to close it out and make time for her family. Those events brought a time of real growth for Angela as a person.

Angela and Carl learned to relate to their businesses without a spirit of competition between them. Both were successful and busy managers of their businesses, but they worked at guarding some time for each other. Both grew personally so they did not outgrow each other. They worked together at building their home and family life. They treated their money as though it belonged to them together regardless of whose earnings it happened to be.

The time demands of each business were so great that the other spouse would have felt neglected if they had not each had their own business and career involvement. Instead, they enjoyed each other and were grateful for the time they did have together. The children felt neglected sometimes, but the Preusses accepted that as a necessary part of building successful businesses which would provide comfortably for the family and fulfill their own personal ego needs for achievement and success.

When Carl had been in his equipment business for six years and Angela had been in home decor products sales for five, it was time for another family move. Their house didn't have enough bedrooms for their family. The children were sleeping three in a room and as they grew that had to be changed. It also became necessary for them to move their residence off the property which was zoned for business use. So in 1962 they bought a lovely home in the middle income area of Patchogue. They have continued to live in that house, even though their income could have made it easily possible for them to have a much more imposing house in a more prestigious residential area. Over the years the Preusses have improved their house and the landscaping of their grounds, so they chose to stay there. They liked the neighborhood and their neighbors. The location was convenient to their businesses so they have been happy residents of their community through the years.

The Maturing Years

Family life for the Preusses, as for all families, included both successes and frustrations, both joys and sadnesses. Early family vacations were taken in a station wagon in which they carried along food, toys, and sleeping mats for the children. They were not campers, so they stayed nights in motels, but they did not often eat in restaurants. On their travels they carried a small propane stove in the car with them and cooked most of their meals at picnic areas. Vacation trips took them to Canada, to Florida, to the Catskill Mountains, and to many other interesting places. In later years much of their vacation time was spent on the family boat.

Carl and Angela were proud and happy parents from the very time of the birth of their children. Angela enjoyed her role as wife and mother. She did not let herself get into a situation where she felt she had "had it" with her children and just had to get away. Her active involvement in her career probably helped her keep from going through phases of annoyance with the daily routines of motherhood and homemaking. Her personal philosophy in raising children is that what matters most is not "the hours you put in" but "what you put into the hours."

Angela and Carl always had high aspirations for the cultural rearing of their children. They surrounded them with books by Dr. Seuss and others. They provided a full spectrum of opportunities in such things as active religious training, swimming lessons, music lessons, and scouting. The parents encouraged and participated with their children in a wide variety of activities.

Through their growing years, Angela gave her children love, guidance, and the benefits of the family's affluent income. But she did not let her prosperity cause her to pass off her responsibilities for homemaking chores. She taught values to her children, often using wise sayings she had gotten from her own mother. Carl and Angela were always careful about their children's friends. They developed and cherished a real closeness in the family, and that closeness still continues, so they share a lot of time together with each other and with their friends included.

The Preuss children were reared to earn their own allowances by doing chores and sharing in the family's house and yard work. Deborah learned early to bake and sew, and she learned from her mother to love doing those things. Angela sewed clothes for her family in order to save money; she did needlework to make lovely things for the house before she could afford to buy them; and she was a thrifty homemaker who did her baking at home and froze foods for the family. As Debbie grew her mother taught her all those helpful household skills. When she was still quite young Debbie became the family baker, and because she learned as a girl to do it well and to love doing it, she has continued to be an excellent baker of homemade goods.

Angela taught Debbie to sew and by the time she was a teenager she was sewing her own clothes. As a young adult she chose to study and learn the art of quilting. When she was Brownie Scout age, Angela joined her in scouting. She was very active in the indoor activities of scouting because she loved the indoor arts and crafts work with the girls. Later, when the scouting program became more involved with outdoor campcraft, Angela dropped out. She did not enjoy camping activities, and her business was demanding more and more of her time as it grew.

As a young girl Debbie was quiet and somewhat shy. In senior high school she decided to take up public speaking and she really bloomed through that training and experience. She developed a very adventuresome spirit, touring Europe and the United States with a group of peers. In college she trained to be a teacher, but chose to go into party-plan selling with her mother instead. She became successful at it before going into the insurance industry as a specialist in estate planning for a brief time. Then she returned to party-plan selling.

David was a quiet boy, but a very determined and ambitious one. He had to work very hard to achieve his goals in school. When anyone asked him why he worked so hard in school, he replied that he was keeping up with his friends. And he did. He stayed in the top ten per cent of his class all through his school years.

When David was thirteen years old his mother challenged him to earn and save fifty dollars by promising to match it with fifty dollars more if he would. He got himself a paper route, delivered papers before going to school in the morning, collecting the money in the afternoons, and in three months he saved the fifty dollars. He proved to her that he could do it, and he also claimed the fifty dollars she had promised. David was very selective in his choice of a college, but he has not made his profession in the field of his training. He has instead chosen to join his father in the family business and proved himself as an excellent professional businessman.

Donald was the most strong-willed and rebellious of the three Preuss children. He was not sneaky, however, but was quite open with his mischief. He was a lover of the outdoors and artistic in spirit. He loved to create works of art from driftwood; he has

26

become a collector of antiques; and while still a young man he carefully framed a scarf his grandfather had brought from Europe as an immigrant to America.

Donald chose to be a music major in college. Once he made that decision he was really motivated, for when he had made up his mind about something he has always worked hard at it. In adulthood Donald has taken up organic gardening; he is very ecologically concerned; and he is an environmental activist. Like David, he has also joined their father in the family business. Carl is very proud of his two sons, who are operating one of the branch stores of the company.

With the teenage years there came teenage problems for the family. Their adolescent years brought real frustrations to Angela because as she began to lose control over her children she was not ready to deal with that changing phase of their relationships. She was not ready to let them become independent adults, free from parental control, no longer dependent on her and Carl. But that was a lesson she had to learn.

Once when Debbie was a teenager she ran away from home. She got into conflict with her parents over a love affair they thought was too premature, but she wasn't ready to listen and give it up. So she ran away to her aunt's house where she stayed for a few days through the hurting time until they could work out a family reconciliation.

During teenage years David developed a habit of heavy beer drinking. One night his teen-crowd took his mother's car for a joyride and it was "totaled" in an accident. Fortunately there were no injuries. For more than a year David covered up the fact that one of the girls and not he was driving when the accident happened. David took the blame instead of letting the guilty girl take it, for he knew it was wrong for them to be drinking beer while they were driving.

Donald's teenage "vice" was smoking marijuana. Carl and Angela were strongly opposed to his experimenting with the drug but he was rebellious and defiant. When he was a child he had been openly mischievous. As a teenager he did not try to hide his activities because he did not think there was anything wrong with what he was doing.

He continued to ignore the rules of the family home about smoking marijuana until Carl and Angela had to confront him and tell him to move out because of what they considered his disrespect.

Donald stayed away from their home for four months before he returned to apologize and become part of the family again.

Except for the brief alienation times during teenage years, the Preuss children were never away from home until they went away to college. So when Debbie went away to Danbury State College, Angela had her first experience of "cutting the apron strings" to let one of her children leave home. That was a very painful experience for her, and it left her feeling really blue for many days before she began to accept it and move on about life with positive enthusiasm.

Seeing David take off on his own was not so painful. He chose to go to the Florida Institute of Technology to study marine biology. His determined pursuit of excellence in school and his careful selection of a college left Carl and Angela with a feeling of confidence about him. While they missed him from the family, they were sure he would do successfully the things he had planned to do.

Donald chose to study music at Stoney Brook University nearby on Long Island. He really put himself into his music training for he loved it. He was not far away from the family during his college years, and by that time Carl and Angela had become rather well adjusted to their fledglings leaving the family nest.

Debbie and David have married and established their own homes, but neither has any children at this time. Donald and David have returned to make Patchogue their home and to join their father in business. The Preusses are proud of their children and grateful for their maturity in adulthood. They believe a loving home environment which included encouragement and high expectations has played an important part in helping their children achieve their successful development into responsible and admirable adults.

Death Invades the Larger Family

As Carl and Angela's children grew up, their parents grew older. The children were still young when their first grandparent died. Angela's father died on September 10, 1958. He died at home, a victim of cancer. Angela and her mother were with him at the time of his death. That was a traumatic grief experience for Angela, and as death so often does, it created in her a sense of anger for the loss which his death brought.

To the end of his life, Angela's father had continued his love for the classics in literature and music. As he read he would underline passages he thought were particularly beautiful. At the time of his death he was engaged in reading John Milton's *Paradise Lost,* so his family chose to have that volume buried with him.

Carl's family had also been an involved and influential part of the Preuss family. His parents like hers were immigrants. Carl and his parents were natives of Germany. Four older brothers were born into the family before the father emigrated to America. Mrs. Preuss was pregnant with Carl at the time the father left for the United States. He came on ahead with the two older brothers, leaving the mother to follow with the rest of the family as soon as possible. When passage was gotten for the others, however, it turned out that ten-year-old Werner was not permitted to come to America because of the effects of a childhood disease. He was left with an aunt in Germany when Mrs. Preuss with Arnold and Carl came to join the other members of the family in New York. Carl grew up with his family in the Bronx before they moved to the Long Island farm where he lived when he met and married Angela.

Carl's older brother Arnold was drafted into the United States Army during World War II and was killed accidentally while in military service. The older brother Werner who had been left in Germany was drafted into the German Army, and he was captured by the American forces. He was brought to America as a prisoner-of-war. One day his mother was reading the lists of names of German prisoners in this country, and there she discovered her son's name. She verified with the Red Cross that it was indeed her son, so she set out to go to Mississippi to visit him, and Carl went with her. Think, if you will, about the agony that mother must have experienced during those years. She had been separated from Werner for years; she had lost her son Arnold who died in military service; she now learned that Werner was a prisoner-of-war. But out of that agony and fear there must have leaped up hope at the idea of seeing Werner again. Maybe the family could be reunited.

Mrs. Preuss and Carl went to see him. Carl was fifteen at the time, and it was the first time he remembered seeing his older brother, for Carl had been a little child when he came to America. They did have a visit with him, but a mother's dream that she might keep her son with her was not to be. After the war ended Werner was required to return to Germany. He chose to stay there and continue to make it his home instead of coming back to join his family in the United States.

Carl's father died in 1959, and in 1961 his mother came to live in the home with Carl and Angela. Since they had three children in the house already, they were quite crowded until they moved to a larger house the next year. There they converted the garage into an apartment for her, and she continued to live with her son and his family until her death on January 27, 1971. After her death they converted the garage apartment into an office for Angela's business. At last they moved her desk out of the corner of their dining room.

Carl and Angela Preuss were strong people because they came from a heritage of strong people. They built a strong marriage based on firm commitments and devoted love. They built a strong family based on the principles of love, responsibility, and shared hard work. Angela's successful business career has been vitally intertwined with her roles as wife and mother in the Carl Preuss family.

Chapter III

Climbing a Career Ladder

The early jobs in the potato fields, the ice cream parlor, and the state mental hospital were but preludes to Angela's career in party-plan sales. Those work experiences included lessons which she learned well, however, and she adapted them and used them in her sales career.

Angela was attracted to party-plan selling because that line of work permitted her to be with her pre-school children during the day. She did her shows and sold her products at home parties in the evening while Carl could be home with the children. Her primary motivation for going to work in a sales career was a need to earn money to supplement the family income. She wanted to earn enough money for the family to get out of the uncomfortable position of being poor. She wanted her family to have a comfortable degree of prosperity. She had a driving determination to make sure she did not live out her life in poverty.

Her Brief Career in Household Products Sales

Angela was recruited for her first job in party-plan sales by a lady named Gertrude Klein. Having such a grand lady as her first supervisor was especially helpful to Angela. She counts it as her third most important blessing, surpassed only by the good fortune to have good parents and a good family.

Gertrude Klein was a devout Christian lady. She was reared in an orphanage as a ward of the state. At age eighteen when it was time for her to leave the orphanage, she married, and she went to work at the very beginning of her adult life in party-plan sales. Her first work was with Stanley Home Products, but later she changed to White Cross Home Products and became a manager who did sales, recruiting, training, and managing. Mrs. Klein was a good teacher and she trained Angela well. Her training and encouragement helped Angela get off to a good start, so she became a top producer of sales for the company in a very short time.

Mrs. Klein's procedure for training was to have Angela make a list of six friends who might host parties for her. Mrs. Klein went with Angela to visit those friends at "coffee-interviews"to persuade them to hold parties and help Angela get started as a dealer. She also "hostess-coached" them in ways to have a good party which would turn out profitably for them and for Angela. By demonstrating an effective party-booking technique, Gertrude Klein helped lay a good beginning foundation for Angela's work in party-plan sales.

After Mrs. Klein had worked with the first five people on Angela's list, and demonstrated how to enlist hostesses and help them prepare a good party, she then let Angela do the booking interview with the sixth person while she observed to see how well Angela could do it.

Mrs. Klein coached Angela never to ask a prospective hostess if she would like to hold a party. That approach leaves an option for declining. The approach should be more positive. Assume that the person wants to have a party and earn the hostess gifts which are available. Suggest a choice between two or three times, such as, "Which would be better for you, Thursday of next week, or Tuesday of the following week?" This discourages the person from declining and helps her make up her mind to book the party with you.

She also trained Angela to memorize her opening talk for enlisting hostesses and for doing party showings so she would make a good impression. People's confidence in you will increase if you show from the beginning that you know what you're doing. Their confidence in their ability to be successful will increase if you show that you can help them do the thing right. Gertrude Klein understood those things about working with people and she taught them to Angela from the very beginning of her career in selling. Angela was a good learner and an apt follower, so she learned and applied the secrets which later helped her become a good leader.

Some of Angela's teenage experiences were also useful to her as she learned effective ways to work with people in party-plan selling. She had learned from practical experience with her mother that you get more positive answers through positive presentations. Say

32

what you say expecting an affirmative answer. Angela was ready to hear that guidance when Gertrude Klein told her that was the way to book parties and make sales. Angela had also learned through the experience of losing her job at the ice cream parlor that it is important to follow instructions carefully when you are being trained or supervised by someone who knows more about the business you are in than you do. So Angela was ready to listen to Mrs. Klein and learn from her the clues to successful party-plan work.

Mrs. Klein really stressed the importance of booking future parties. It was her theory that bookings for future parties gotten at a party are more important than the sales of that particular party. She taught Angela that a big party with no bookings is the way out of the party-plan business. This early conditioning about the importance of booking future parties became a key to Angela's success. She always made sure she booked future parties at every showing, and then she compounded those times into opportunities to make sales and book still more parties.

Angela's work with White Cross Home Products had a very undesirable feature for her. The White Cross sales program required the dealers to sell, collect, package, and deliver the products. Angela found the additional responsibility of packaging and delivering the products she had sold to be a problem. The added work often kept her busy day and night, and at one time it caused her to interrupt her selling career because of the home-making demands of three young children and a house to keep. When she resumed her selling career, it was with another company and the circumstances were very different.

Beginning of Her Career
In Home Decor Products Sales

Coppercraft Guild put a new face on party-plan work for Angela. In February, 1957, Gertrude Daniels called Angela and wanted to interview her about becoming a counselor (the name used by that company for its dealers) in home decor products sales. Angela replied that she was not interested because she was too busy with three preschool children, ages four, three, and nine months. Mrs. Daniels persisted. She told Angela about a new party-plan approach being used by her company which did not involve those who sell in the packaging and delivery work. At that idea Angela fairly burst with excitement, and said, "You mean I would just have to sell!" To her that sounded like Utopia after her experience with White Cross, so she agreed to take the job.

Angela went into business selling the home decor product line with considerable uncertainty. The basic inventory of products at that time ranged from towel rings at $2.50 to ice buckets at $14.95. She was afraid the products were too expensive, so that she would not be able to make a go of it selling those luxury items among her circle of acquaintances.

Nevertheless she felt driven to join Gertrude Daniels' sales group. Her family needed some additional income rather desperately because Carl had just gone into his equipment business and it was not yet showing much profit for family living expenses. In addition, party-plan selling was a field in which she already had some experience, but she did not know of another party-plan company at that time which did not involve the sellers in packaging and delivery work. All the factors combined to persude Angela to take Gertrude Daniels' offer, so she signed on as a counselor with Coppercraft Guild on March 27, 1957.

Gertrude Daniels did not do an effective job of orientation and training for her new product line as Gertrude Klein had done for Angela when she began to sell the household products line. Mrs. Daniels remembered Angela as a top producer of sales for White Cross, and perhaps she did not think she needed training because of that earlier experience. Whatever her reasons, she merely brought the demonstrator cases by to Angela and left her to figure out alone what to do with them.

The first six weeks were very discouraging to her. The first paycheck Angela received was for only $9.00 because of the small sales at her first shows. She went on to hold seventeen shows before she received her first bonus check, which was based on sales exceeding $600 in a month. Her seventeenth show was her first one to have sales of more than $100. Angela was about ready to call it quits. Then two things happened.

Her manager was concerned that Angela's sales were so low. In talking with her, she discovered that Angela was in fact killing opportunities for sales by the way she went about booking future shows. Angela had been so conditioned to put bookings before sales that she actually discouraged sales in order to get people to book a show. When someone would look interestedly at an item that was being demonstrated, Angela would say, "Don't buy it. Have a show and you can get it free as a hostess gift." Needless to say, many of them didn't buy. She needed to learn a new approach.

Mrs. Daniels suggested that she go to a show and watch Connie Verin do a demonstration. She did, and she discovered an important clue to success. Connie held each of the beautiful items she demonstrated as though she loved it. She presented her products with obvious respect for their beauty and quality. Angela caught a new idea, so she set out to develop the new approach she needed.

Angela went to work to get really well acquainted with the products she was trying to sell. She researched the history, the uses, and the characteristics of copper. Her study helped her become thoroughly familiar with the qualities of the products she demonstrated at her shows. She went to work also to develop some real expertise in the field of home decoration. She gathered ideas from all the best home-oriented magazines and developed a scrapbook full of decorator ideas which she had on display at her shows. People could look over the room decoration schemes she had for them to examine and get ideas for using items she demonstrated to enhance the beauty of their own homes.

Angela used the decorator schemes herself to plan her shows. She developed a pattern of demonstrating her products in groups according to their use in the home. Three categories became the framework of her shows for she arranged her products into items to decorate the home, items to enhance gracious living, and items of fashion jewelry. She displayed her products in those categories and developed a continuity in her presentation so there would be a smooth flow from one category to another and from one item to another.

Since homes are the environment in which party-plan selling is done, Angela let the home guide her in the development of her presentations. The first thing you see when you enter a home is the plants, so she began her demonstration with the planters. From there she went on to other decorative ideas until she had covered her home decoration category. When she was ready to show the serving utensils, Angela put them into a very romantic setting by changing the mood and showing them by candlelight in lovely table settings.

Angela developed a technique by emphasizing product groupings and matching pieces. She then encouraged people to buy one of a set or a group at the show and buy the matching pieces at later shows, or buy one piece and hold a party to get matching pieces free as hostess gifts. This new approach worked for her. Sales and bookings began to grow. Angela was on her way!

As she became an effective demonstrator, her paychecks grew. Angela got excited and enthusiastic about her success with her new company. She was beginning to be aware that there is a science to profitable party-plan selling. Years later she compared herself to Dorothy in *The Wizard of Oz* who believed that by following a yellow brick road she could find the wonderful wizard who could make her dreams come true. Angela believed she had found the first of those "yellow bricks" on which she could walk to find her "wizard" and the answers to her dreams. In her excitement she began to talk to other people to persuade them to get into the interesting and profitable work of party-plan selling. Without realizing it, she was becoming a recruiter; and without being aware of it she had taken her first steps onto the path which led her into management and upward in her amazing career.

Angela learned four keys to success as a party-plan seller during those early days. Those keys are equally applicable to success in direct sales in programs other than party-plan and with products other than home decor items. Those keys are:

Key # 1 – Believe In Your Product And In Your Company. After getting well acquainted with the products she was selling, Angela fell in love with them. She was convinced without any doubt whatever that the products were of good quality, they were well worth their prices, and they would enhance the beauty of the homes of people who owned them.

She was also sold on her company's approach, which included generous hostess gifts to make holding parties attractive. The company's program for their demonstrators offered an opportunity to write your own paycheck through commissions and bonuses based on sales.

But there was more. Angela Preuss believed in the quality of the products she offered for sale; she believed in the company she represented; but she also believed in herself. She was convinced that she could enlist hostesses, hold shows, do demonstrations, sell products, and make attractive money doing it.

Key # 2 – Be Enthusiastic. Enthusiasm requires a positive and optimistic attitude. Only so long as the flame of enthusiasm is kept burning can success be achieved, but enthusiasm is like a flame also in that when it burns it ignites. Enthusiasm generates the energy which creates more enthusiams and which produces the achievements of life. Enthusiasm stirs the interest of others so they are attracted to buy a product or "buy in on" a venture. Positive enthusiasm is essential in party-plan selling to book parties, to sell products, to enlist recruits to join you in selling, and to motivate colleagues in their pursuit of super achievements. Angela Preuss has been a person who through good times and bad would not let the flame of enthusiasm die. She has provided an enthusiastic example and encouragement to the people who have worked with her and under her supervision throughout her business career.

Key # 3 – Present Your Products Attractively. Angela learned to do this by candlelight shows and well-planned demonstrations. Every line of products has its own distinctive characteristics and its own distinctive uses. Angela had to learn that selling lovely home decor products was different from selling household products for everyday use and housecleaning. The presentation has to fit the product, and once she learned that, her sales began to really increase.

In party-plan sales it is also essential to emphasize the benefits that can be had for holding parties, for securing hostess bookings is the way a party-plan seller stays in business. The shows themselves are a part of the product you must sell. Angela developed an effective technique for doing her shows, and she also developed an effective technique for using "opinion slips" to discover leads for enlisting hostesses, getting referrals, and recruiting other demonstrators to join her sales organization.

Key # 4 – Sell People As Well As Products. When Angela began to succeed, the thrill of success was delightful to her. She wanted to share her good fortune with others. Before she ever dreamed of advancing into management and making money by her recruiting efforts, Angela began to talk to other people about becoming party-plan salespersons so they could get in on the good thing she had discovered. Her interest in selling people on a good idea was the thing that led Angela to take her first step up the ladder into management. She was about to make another step down the yellow brick road in her search for the wizard of success.

Growth into Management

Angela's unit manager at that time noticed her enthusiasm for selling other people on the idea of getting into party-plan sales. She suggested to her that if she would recruit five people to become counselors, she would receive her own attache case as a bonus and she would also become a district manager. That idea seemed incredible to Angela. She was afraid to make that move and launch out on such an undertaking. After all, she had only a high school education; she had had no training or experience in managing people; and she had three small children at home to be responsible for. The manager didn't give up, however, for she believed Angela could make it. She pointed out to Angela that her responsibilities as a district manager would be to recruit her people and then pass on to them printed materials which came from the company with information and suggestions.

After considerable persuasion, Angela finally agreed with reluctance and with real reservation in her own mind. She didn't really know whether management was "her thing" or whether she could handle it within the time she could devote after caring for her homemaking responsibilities. But the motivation to be a winner was strong in her and she launched out on a career adventure, not dreaming at that time where it would eventually take her. The yellow brick road was inviting, but a little foreboding for it was unfamiliar, and she didn't know much about the wizard she was searching for.

As Angela moved one step up the career ladder into her first management responsibilities, she discovered that six additional features were essential for her effective achievement as a district manager. Those six features of first level management were:

Feature # 1 – Good Work Habits. Most people who work in party-plan sales work out of their homes. Most of the people who work in the first levels of management in the industry also work from their homes. Angela was a very normal party-plan person in that regard. She worked from her home and had to deal with the advantages and disadvantages of doing so. A pattern of work habits had to be developed for her to have an established division of her time between household chores, personal and family time, her business, and community projects. Working from home requires personal discipline to get the job done for so many other things are

38

at hand waiting to be attended to. Working from the home also means you are always on the job and rarely do you "close up shop" and get away from it. Good work habits are essential to give your job proper attention and at the same time keep it from encroaching on home life too much. Her advance into management increased that need for good work habits for Angela.

Feature # 2 – Organization. An "office corner" was necessary for organizing business schedules and materials. While Angela was only a counselor, she could keep most of her materials in her demonstrator cases. After she became a district manager she had records to keep, materials to distribute, and other business items. The requirement she faced was to keep it all together so she could do her work, and at the same time to keep it from invading the whole house.

Angela worked from a desk, some makeshift files, and a bookcase all set up in a corner of the dining room. That corner became her office when she was a district manager. It continued to serve as her office until after she was an area manager and her unit's annual sales were exceeding a million dollars. Careful organization and efficiency made it possible.

Feature # 3 – Self-Discipline. A part of Angela's pattern of work habits involved a system of uninterrupted work periods. She found that she could accomplish more in one hour of concentrated work than she could in four hours of "stop and go" activity. Angela's way of having uninterrupted work times was by use of an imaginary time-clock. According to a time schedule she had determined was best for her, she "punched in" and worked without interruption for a planned period until time to "punch out" and stop.

Such a work system required considerable self-discipline on her part. As a mother with her three small children she had to set her work times when the children were asleep, at school, or being cared for by someone else. So schedules were subject to change, and that required flexibility and even more self-discipline by her. Management responsibilities added to her work load and increased even more her need for self-discipline.

Feature # 4 – Self-Starting Motivation. Working from her home as a district manager required Angela to be her own primary motivator. It was no problem for her, however, because she was so enthusiastic and ambitious. She hurried through her morning household chores so she could get to her business activities. There were shows to book and plan for; recruiting contacts to be made; and counselors to train and motivate. Angela had a district to manage and enlarge, and it was her disposition to be involved in everything that was going on in that unit. She wanted every party and every promotion to mean as much as possible for every one of her people.

Angela describes her approach to management as S.T.P. — See The People. She used the telephone very little in booking shows or recruiting counselors. The person-to-person approach worked better for her, for then she could show samples of her products and of the hostess gifts which were available. She went to interview prospective recruits personally, and after new counselors had been enlisted Angela would have them come to her home where she would train them in effective party-plan sales techniques.

The first unit level manager in a party-plan sales company must be a self-starter, for that person must generate personal motivation and develop productive enthusiasm in the people who hold the party showings and market the company products to the consumers. Angela sensed the importance of that role for her success in management, so she went to work to develop the skills necessary for keeping herself and her people actively motivated toward superior achievements.

Feature # 5 – Initiative. When Angela joined Coppercraft Guild, the company was still young. When she became a unit manager she discovered there was available very little in the way of training materials for new recruits in the sales units. She took the initiative to put the sales knowledge she had acquired into written form. By investing in an inexpensive duplicator, she was able to prepare papers on "How To Do Bookings", "What Are the Secrets of Effective Recruiting?" and "Show Techniques That Work" for use in training her counselors. In that way she provided her people with written answers to the objections they would meet to party-plan sales, to the problems they would have to deal with in working out of their homes, and to the keys for success in home-party sales.

Angela learned quickly that having available such training and support materials as these would enhance her efficiency as a manager and motivator of people, so she took the personal initiative and prepared them for her own use with her people. Over a period of time she prepared the materials she needed and compiled them into a training manual, which later became the foundation document for development of a counselor information guide that was used throughout the company. A principle of effective leadership was being applied here: see a need and take the initiative to find or produce resources which will adequately meet that need.

Feature # 6 – Managing People. The first step up the management ladder in the party-plan sales industry is the management of a small group of people who find hostess homes, hold home shows where they demonstrate their line of products, and makes sales among the group of people gathered for the showing. Angela's district unit began with seven counselors. She did not take over an established unit which someone else had formed and trained. The unit was formed when she recruited and trained the seven people. She was a new manager, having had no previous experience in supervising other workers. Her people were newly recruited into party-plan sales work. Angela had to learn her way along in management as she was helping them get started booking shows, doing demonstrations, selling products, keeping records, and making reports.

But Angela has something going for her. She is a person who likes people, so she has a tendency to get involved in their lives and make their problems her problems. As a result, she stayed close to her people, communicated regularly with them, and was available to help them get going in their new work. She had to learn, however, that while she could help them solve their booking and selling problems, and she could help them manage the business administration needs of their work, she could not solve their family and health problems. Early in her management career she got too involved in the personal problems of some of her people, but she learned it was not wise to let that happen.

The approach she developed was to be understanding and encouraging with people who had personal problems, and not to put pressure on them to produce sales while they were struggling with those problems. In her business promotion Angela concentrated on working with people who could produce, and waited until things changed for troubled people so they would be able to dig in again to work on their production and sales. Then she would get involved to give guidance and encouragement to help them get their business momentum rolling again.

By aggressive and effective recruiting and management the district grew from seven to fifty counselors. That successful growth opened an opportunity for Angela to advance from district manager to regional manager. At that level of management it would be her responsibility to work with a hundred people. Again the idea frightened her at first. She had become comfortable with the scope of her responsibility as a district manager, for she worked with a group of people she had recruited and trained personally. Could she really handle the larger responsibility of regional management? The only way to know was to try it. Angela's basic ambition came through, so she decided to accept the challenge and become a regional manager.

Management Responsibility Expands

Added responsibility always brings some changes in a person's style of life. It always involves doing some things you have not done previously, and many times it involves giving up some things you have been doing. Both were true for Angela. As she devoted more time to the rewarding activities of her career, she dropped out of some of the community projects to which she had given time in earlier years. She also gave up some of the "chore work" of both home and business. Family income was sufficient at last for her to have a part-time housekeeper and a part-time secretary.

Her workload was as great as ever, however, but as a regional manager she was more involved in managerial activities than she had been before. She found three expanded features in her responsibilities at the new level of management. They were:

Requirement # 1 – Broader Communication. As a district manager the scope of her communication requirement was to deal with her own local unit, all of whom were relatively nearby and with whom she had regular face-to-face meetings. As a regional manager she had responsibility to communicate with more people spread over a larger territory, and more of her work had to be done through district managers. She had to motivate district managers to motivate the counselors in their districts. She needed an expanded communication tool, so she began to publish a regional paper for all the people in her regional units. Angela called her paper the *Preuss*

42

Press.

Angela used her regional paper to give recognition to personal achievements in sales. She used it to carry on a continuous program of training for her people. She shared success stories so others could profit from new ideas which others proved would work. Motivation was the emphasis she regularly designed into her "Thought Of The Month" column. She occasionally included as a special feature an inspirational story from the life of some person who had achieved outstanding success.

In addition to her regional communication, Angela also was regularly involved in personal communication with many individuals. Special attention was given to encouraging newly recruited counselors. Welcome letters were sent to them, along with information about the history of their company and the great variety of uses their products had. Angela worked at helping them become familiar with their new company and their new line of products so they could appreciate the quality of those products and demonstrate them effectively at their shows. Personal attention was also given to special days in the lives of the individual people within the region. She sent birthday cards to all her people; she sent notes of congratulation or encouragement; and occasionally she sent flowers at very special times. Angela tried very hard to make all her people feel special and appreciated.

Requirement # 2 – Continued Development. Solid growth is more important than rapid growth, but steady growth is essential for building a business and a successful company. Angela majored on identifying and encouraging super-achievers. She was constantly on a "recruiting search" for additional people with potential to develop as managers who could expand the regional team. One of her recruiting techniques was to hold periodic "manageramas". At her first one she had eighty manager candidates, who were invited to that special event with their spouses. There Angela presented the management story of their company and distributed information folders which outlined district manager qualifications, responsibilities, and benefits. Her program of recruitment and training for managers was both aggressive and thorough. She wanted more managers, for that was essential to the continued growth of her region, but she wanted them to be well-trained and effective so they would make a contribution to her goal of continued development. As a regional manager Angela carried on a perennial program of updating the training and motivation of her working managerial personnel. She gave regular attention to helping her established managers as well as to the recruitment and training of new managers. And her regional organization did grow. By 1966 her region was made up of ten districts with one hundred forty counselors, and at that time the region was doing annual sales of half-a-million dollars.

Requirement # 3 – Response To Greater Challenges. Jim Pollard was the manager of the area to which Angela's region belonged. He proved to be a very helpful influence to her because he believed in her and he motivated her by giving her significant challenges. He recognized her potential for leadership and sought to bring it out by encouraging her to set high goals and work to reach them. He challenged her to lead her region to increase its sales by one hundred per cent in a single year. That challenge was set before her in terms of a specific goal, to go from half-a-million to more than a million dollars in sales in one year.

Angela thought he was kidding, so at first she did not take his challenge seriously. No major sales effort was made toward reaching that goal during the first half of the year 1967. By June, however, she learned that Jim Pollard was not kidding at all. He was really quite serious. He really did believe that she could pull it off with her regional unit. She, in turn, felt ashamed that she was letting him down by not even trying. So she began to respond to the challenge and she went to work on reaching that goal.

To reach such an ambitious goal she would have to motivate a positive and enthusiastic response to the challenge from all the people in the districts of her region, and they would have to work doubly hard because they had let the first half of the year go by before starting to work on doubling their sales. Angela began by breaking down the total goal into proportionate district goals which she distributed to the thirteen district managers who were then in the region.

The challenge began to catch them up in it as they began to catch the fire of her enthusiasm and determination. Angela left no stone unturned and no detail unattended to during the last half of that year. She organized and promoted their drive toward the goal down to the very last minute of the year. Everyone was encouraged to hold special end-of-the-year shows, and Angela developed a plan to have all the last minute orders collected and hand-carried to the home office on the last day of the year. They reached the goal by exceeding a million dollars in regional sales in a single year for the first time in the history of the company.

They exceeded their goal by only $57 and everybody took a great deal of pride in the achievement. Their total goal was large but that $57 order could have been the sales of any individual counselor in the region, for if anyone of them had come up short in sales by just that one amount, then the million dollar goal would not have been reached.

Angela had responded to the challenge of becoming a regional manager. She had proven her ability to manage a larger unit with more people in it. The effectiveness of her managerial ability and of her leadership of people was demonstrated by leading her region to such a remarkable sales goal of doubling sales in a single year and reaching the million dollar level. The result of her signal success as a regional manager was her advancement to area manager in 1968.

Even Larger Challenges

Sometimes clouds come with challenges, to make them even more difficult to handle and master. Angela found it so in the very early days of her work as an area manager. Her life and work took on a new face in three different areas. They were:

Facet # 1 – Need To Have Faith When Others Are Frustrated. Coppercraft Guild was merged with a parent company West Bend Products. Soon thereafter an executive management decision was made which put the counselors and managers in the company into frustrated disarray. A new hostess plan was initiated which designated other company products as hostess premiums instead of the desirable decor products which had been given previously. That decision turned out to be disastrous to their show bookings, for the other products were simply not as attractive to potential hostesses as the lovely home decor items from the company's main product line.

Faith and perseverance became the need of the day. The people in the field needed to believe that they could survive in spite of the change in company policy. They also needed the stamina to stick it out while they worked and hoped for a change in the hostess gift plan. Fortunately after six months a change was made and the standard product line hostess gifts were reinstated. It was a traumatic situation for Angela during her first year as an area manager. It tested her ability to deal with problems in a broad area. She learned from that experience to have faith in her ability to help her people keep their bearings through troubled times. Coping with such a challenge, and managing it successfully helped her develop additional strength which in turn helped her achieve even greater successes.

Facet # 2 – Expanded Involvement And Its Accompanying Changes. One of Angela's responsibilities as an area manager was the development of new markets. That role required her to travel a great deal more, to find key people with managerial ability, and to organize expansion into new territories.

The travel involved brought significant changes into her marriage. Neither she nor Carl liked their being apart, but they accepted it as a part of the cost involved in her expanded opportunity and increased responsibility. Her travel brought a whole new dimension of loneliness into her life and Carl's, however, and it necessitated having a full-time housekeeper and cook for the family. Fortunately the strength of their marriage, which was a product of their building through the years, was sufficient to sustain the change and make the adjustment of life style which her new job level involved.

Angela was quite effective in discovering the people needed for the expansion of their home decor product market into new areas. She recruited the people, trained them for their responsibilities, organized the operation of the sales organization in the new territory, and accomplished a marked increase in the area she was managing. She could sell party-plan programs and home decor products in the phenomenal way because she could sell herself so well.

Facet # 3 – New Ventures In Promotion. As an area manager it fell Angela's lot to make a new travel incentive program work within the company. Opportunities were given to win expense-paid trips to conventions through sales contests. The objective was to motivate people throughout the organization to really push themselves to hold larger product shows in their efforts to win the contests and the prizes.

Angela promoted the incentive contests in her area very energetically. She used creative promotional themes based on the location of a particular convention. To stir interest in a Miami national convention, for instance, she went to Florida, had her picture made in front of the convention hotel, and mailed it with a promotional message to all her managers during a cold wintry February. That really sparked their interest in trying to win a trip to sunny Miami for the convention.

Another of their conventions was held in the Bahamas. They chose to call it the "Yellow Bird" convention, so Angela kicked off her promotion of a contest for free trips to that convention by sending all her managers a live canary with cage and a poem which read, "This yellow bird has come to say, 'Are your recruits on their way?' If this is so, O glory be, And I will sing 'Come fly with me, To the Bahamas.' "

Being near the top level of management for the company, Angela began to have opportunities to help plan conventions. She applied her creative imagination to the task to help make those events great occasions which would attract lots of attention and interest. She arranged to have hula girls and fire dancers at a convention in Hawaii. Windmills and Dutch dancers helped build the theme atmosphere she planned for a convention in Amsterdam, Holland. At a Disney World convention she secured from Eastern Airlines the entire Mickey Mouse Review on stage. And at a June convention she arranged for every person in the Preuss Division who had made an organizational management advancement during the year to march into the convention hall robed in caps and gowns to the music of "Pomp and Circumstance."

These promotions helped enhance interest among the company people to increase sales and become more involved in company activities. Pride in accomplishment, and pride in leadership advancement were features upon which those promotional events were developed. They were new ventures for Angela, but she quickly became quite good at it, adding to her success and to the success of the company.

Angela's effectiveness as an area manager and as a company promoter brought her to another new level of responsibility. In 1972, Angela Preuss was promoted to divisional vice-president, a new executive position in the company which had been created for her to recognize and reward her achievements.

Executive Responsibility

Angela had worked hard, applying both creativity and enthusiasm to the development of her career in party-plan sales and management. She was following her "yellow brick road" in search of the wizard of success and happiness. She was beginning to be aware that there was no wizard to be found, for the wizard was herself, and the formula for success was to make the most of every "yellow brick" on the road. At each level of advancement she mastered the responsibility of the job and performed it with effectiveness, which in turn led to a next higher level of career opportunity for her. Her promotion to divisional vice-president moved her up from middle management to an executive position in the company.

As with all career advancement, that promotion brought advantages and privileges, but it also brought enlarged and different responsibilities. A luxury company car, an executive title, and a lot of recognition went with the new position.

The position was not new for Angela alone, however, for it was a newly created position, and as such it was new for everybody in the company. Being the first person to fill that office, she had a tremendous responsibility to develop the role of that executive level position within the company structure. That role was envisioned to be a bridge between the sales people in the field and the production people in the factory. Angela had previously been a field person in charge of an extensive sales organization. Now she would have to become aware of and familiar with such things as factory problems, production costs, and inventory management. Her executive position called for her to be involved in helping make company policies, where previously she had been involved in applying those policies in the sales operations of the company. This was a new world of challenge and opportunity for Angela, but the delight of it soon began to wear off and a personal career crisis began to emerge.

Development of New Directions

For twenty-five years the Preuss family had struggled to get ahead. They found their places, they worked hard, and finally they had made it. Carl's business was solid and profitable. Angela had made a lot of money in her sales career. They were out of debt and prosperous. They had the things they had dreamed of, the kinds of things many people dream of having: a house, lovely clothes, luxury cars, a yacht, a family airplane, a full-time housekeeper. Angela mastered the job of company divisional vice-president and turned down an offer to move up and be groomed for the presidency of the company. She had arrived. No more demands, but also no more challenges, and no more goals. It seemed that retirement was the next move for her.

But retire to what? She was only in her mid-forties, so what should she do with the rest of her life? She bought a book entitled *Rehearse Before You Retire* and read it. She set out to follow its suggestions to prepare for retirement by developing new ventures in other areas. For two years Angela searched for that new road, but all the time she was becoming more depressed. Just as she had learned that there was no wizard of success, now she was learning that there is no wizard of happiness. The wizard is you, and you have more to do with making your dreams come true than anybody else. But Angela was not creating conditions of happiness for herself. A mid-career had arisen for her. A hard career decision was imperative.

Angela chose to go back with enthusiasm into the world of party-plan sales where she had found two decades of happy and challenging life. She would forget about retirement, create new goals for herself and fashion for herself the challenge she needed for enthusiasm and happiness in life. She renovated her office, bought new office equipment, started new files, and set herself to project and achieve new goals.

It was 1975 and the Preuss Division was at a level of five million dollars per year in sales. Angela projected a plan to double that level of annual sales in three years. Her goal was to lead her division to advance to TEN MILLION DOLLARS in sales in 1978. That goal was ambitious enough to put challenge into her career again.

New Challenge and Renewed Enthusiasm

Angela had fashioned a challenge which would require her to make effective use of all the knowledge, skill, and enthusiasm she possessed. She had acquired extensive knowledge of party-plan selling through experience in both sales and management. She knew what demonstrators holding shows would have to do to increase their number of parties and their sales. She knew what managers would have to do in recruiting and training in order to add new people to their units and increase the achievements of their people. She knew what regional and area managers would have to do in promotion and motivation to make the cumulative increases which would bring them to their goal. Angela knew all these things by experience for she had performed successfully at every level of the sales organization. And in her challenge campaign she would have to make use of all that knowledge as she planned and directed the drive of the division throughout the three campaign years.

Organizational and promotional skills were also things Angela had acquired through her years of experience. She had effectively built district, regional, and area organizations by her recruiting and training efforts. She had expanded operations into new territories and developed successful sales units there. And throughout her expanding organization Angela had motivated her people with promotional contests, with sales incentives, with bonus travel, and with personal encouragement. In her own managerial development she had become able to organize programs and motivate people to reach phenomenal achievements. In her three-year campaign to achieve a TEN MILLION DOLLAR year, she would have to employ all those skills to the maximum to lead the division to success.

And her own enthusiasm for the challenge would prove to be a crucial factor. Highs and lows are normal features of business cycles, and many people need a source of enthusiastic encouragement to help them recover from the low periods of the cycle. Angela has natural enthusiasm which matches her thirst for challenge, and she has tenacious determination in the face of difficulty. These personal forces she applied with zest in her leadership role toward the goal of a TEN MILLION DOLLAR year.

Angela began by organizing the campaign carefully. By analysis she determined the advances they would need to make each of the first two years. Then she calculated the monthly goals which would take them successfully through the 1978 campaign. That organizational leadership enabled her to give the division the promotional guidance needed to reach their goal.

In 1976 the Preuss Division sold 6.2 million dollars, and in 1977 their sales jumped to 8.4 million dollars. They were well on track when they entered 1978 with their plan to make that year an exciting and impressive climax of the three-year drive.

Severe winter weather caused disastrous disruptions in business schedules and for the first quarter the division fell far behind its pro-rated goals. Discouragement hit hard at many of the people in the organization. Angela had to come through with organized motivation and catch-up programs. She had to develop corrective plans to supplement the over-all campaign plan she had designed for the year. Her creative skills and energetic determination enabled her to give the division the drive it needed to go over its goal down at the very end of the year. They had succeeded!

Success and Celebration

The work of the people had made the division's success possible, so Angela planned a celebration to crown their success with gala festivities. Her knowledge of the motivational impetus of recognition and appreciation enabled her to see that such a celebration would make it easier to enlist their enthusiastic participation in the next promotion she planned. So a spectacular celebration dinner was held for managers from the division and key people throughout the company.

Angela's career in party-plan sales had reached a thrilling apogee of success, recognition, and satisfaction. The rewards had matched her dreams as she led her sales organization to advance from one million to ten million dollars in annual sales in just ten years, 1968-1978.

Ten Reasons Why I Believe in Party-Plan Selling

By Angela Preuss

1. Party-plan selling provides flexibility and enables you to control your own time schedule.

2. Home shows insure that you will be welcomed when you go to a hostess' home by invitation.

3. Home shows and group selling provide opportunity for greater sales volume than one-to-one selling.

4. Home shows provide opportunity for group selling in concentrated periods of time.

5. Home shows encourage initiative in planning and creativity in product demonstrations.

6. Home shows provide opportunity to book future shows which in turn provide prospects for future sales.

7. Commission sales enable you to determine your chosen level of earnings by your own initiative and willingness to work.

8. Party-plan sales provide opportunity for recruiting as well as selling and for advancing into management with its accompanying additional profits.

9. Party-plan sales provide the motivational thrust of incentive bonuses in addition to base sales commissions.

10. The independent business status of party-plan salespeople encourages self-development and high achievement.

Chapter IV

Juggling Life's Pieces

A successful career person like Angela Preuss is often asked questions about how she achieved success and how it has affected her life. Her work in party-plan sales has caused her to work primarily with women, and her success in business and family has caused many of those women to ask her those questions, for they have to deal with many of the same problems she has met and solved. Their respect for her effective leadership and career success is a source of great admiration for her as a woman, so many women who worked with her have wanted to know how she has juggled life's pieces and put them together so well. The questions she has been asked have usually fallen into one of four areas.

Relating Career to Marriage

Since she is a career woman and a wife, Angela is often asked if her husband is jealous of her. The issue raised by that question has two sides. Can a husband tolerate his wife being successful in a career without having his male ego injured by her personal independence of him? And can a woman handle the dual role of a successful career in the competitive world of business and the homemaking responsibilities which go with her role as a wife?

Carl Preuss became a successful businessman in his own right during the same years Angela was building her business organization. Together, during those same years, they were building a family. After thirty years of marriage, with their parental responsibilities behind them, their marriage is solid and each takes great pride in the other. What were the keys which enabled them to develop such a healthy and solid interpersonal relationship?

The foundation of their relationship has been love and devoted commitment to one another and to their marriage. Compatibility and not competition has been the pattern of their living and working together. Because both are ambitious and assertive people, if either had attempted to be dominant over the other it would have caused real problems for them in their marriage.

Their approach has been to work things out together, negotiating and cooperating instead of trying to win out over one another in any differences which arose. They decided together about Carl leaving his railroad job to go into business for himself. They chose together to use Angela's earnings for family expenses while Carl turned his earnings back into the equipment business to capitalize it adequately.

Shared responsibility for the house and the children was developed as a way of life. Carl watched the children at night while Angela did her home shows. Angela scheduled cooking, housekeeping, childcare, and laundry into her daily activities and attended regularly to those homemaking responsibilities while she was still managing a very busy schedule of home shows and business development. And when Angela became so engrossed in her business that Carl suggested she was beginning to love it more than she loved him, she covered her desk with a sheet on Sundays to shut out the business and guard time to spend with her family.

Money management was important to Carl and Angela, for in the early years of their marriage there was little income and they had to manage it carefully to make ends meet. Neither could look for special advantage when both were trying to get their businesses started. Disciplined money management was vital to provide family needs and still allot the needed amounts for putting the family business on solid footing. Later, when money became plentiful for them, they still had to manage the money to keep it from becoming a cause of jealousy between them. They always treated the money as "ours", not as "mine" and "yours".

And their approach worked for them. At the victory celebration following the successful campaign to reach TEN MILLION DOLLARS in sales in 1978, Angela was in the limelight and Carl was right at her side. In his speech of that evening he spoke with obvious pride about his wife and her accomplishments. He described Angela as a good mother and an excellent wife. He described to the gathered crowd how they had worked together and played together. While others talked of her business success, Carl talked of her family success.

Relating Career to the Role of Mother

Her most-often-asked questions about being a mother and a businesswoman concern whether their children were resentful of the time she spent away from them. Angela answers "Yes" to the women who ask that question. She goes on to explain that children are by nature very selfish, and they never like to share their mother with anyone or anything. Children will completely dominate a mother's life and control all of her time if she will let them. Any woman who works outside the home at a job in business or industry can expect her children sometimes to say, "You're never home," or "You're always gone."

To relate a career to the role of motherhood effectively, a woman must search her soul and decide whether what she is doing is constructive or destructive. Is her family being neglected too much? Is she performing adequately on the job or not? Is she too selfish in her motives, or is she so self-effacing that she surrenders her own selfhood to the demands of other family members? These are questions a working career mother must ask and answer honestly if she would make a candid examination of the relationship of her career and domestic roles. Angela asked them of herself, concluded that she could manage both roles, and set out to develop a business career while her family responsibilities were at their greatest.

Of Angela's three children, David was most outspoken in his criticism of her career. As a teenager he expressed resentment of her values, saying that she had given priority to her job and to the things her money could buy. By that time the family did have a yacht, an airplane, and an air-conditioned house. David accused his mother of doing what she did for herself and not for her family. Angela agreed with David that she and Carl had always done some things for themselves, but the interests of the family had always been included and given genuine importance. Angela did use the yacht for business entertainment and promotions, but it was a boat for the family also. The plane was primarily for Carl's hobby but the family shared it. The air-conditioned house did include Angela's office, but the children enjoyed its space and comfort, and they were always free to have their friends in to enjoy it with them.

Once in a training seminar the perennial question was asked of Angela, "Did your children resent your being away so much in your work?" On that occasion her daughter Deborah was present so

Angela replied, "Debbie's here, why not ask her?" Deborah responded, "As children, yes we did sometimes resent the amount of time she spent away at work — but now we wouldn't exchange our mother for any other in the world." That beautiful testimony warmed Angela's heart, as it would have the heart of any mother.

When Carl and Angela's children were small, they established savings accounts for them with money gifts that were received at birthdays and on other special occasions. Family resources were quite limited in those years, and those savings accounts were their hope that the children would be able to go to college when they grew up. Only after they were mature did the children understand that depth of concern their parents had had for them. By the time the children were ready for college, however, the family income was sufficient that the savings did not have to be used for college expenses.

Angela explained to her children, just as she has often explained to people in career seminars, that there are different kinds of mothers because the women who are mothers have differing needs as persons, and their families have differing needs also. Some mothers are career women, some are socialites, and some are just simply homebodies. Angela emphasizes that it is OK for each woman to be the kind of mother her own personal needs and those of her family indicate, but she also tries to help women understand that children will grow up and leave home, and an "empty nest" can become a very lonely place for someone whose life has been wrapped up completely in her children.

Children's needs are important, but personal needs are important also. A person who has aptitude and interest in being a career person can be very unhappy if that personal need is not satisfied, and a person who is unhappy in herself will not make others around her happy. Angela worked hard to make sure the needs, but not necessarily the individual personal desires, of her family were always met. But she was the kind of mother who did not neglect the cultivation of her own personal needs to satisfy her ambition for career and financial success. As her children matured into adulthood, they accepted Angela for the kind of mother she is, and they affirm her as a good mother and a successful career person at the same time.

Identifying the Keys to Her Success

People ask Angela, "How did you make it to the top?" "How did you as a woman become a vice-president of a major national company?" "Was it luck?" "What did you do differently from what others have done?" She insists that it was not a mere stoke of luck. Angela attributes her success to applying effective principles and sticking with an effective program.

Carl and Angela both believe in perseverance. They stayed with the task of building their businesses, and they worked hard at it week after week and year after year. They invested themselves in what they were doing, they had a lot at stake, so they would not walk away in the face of difficulties when they arose. A good demonstration of their tenacity came during a holiday crisis.

It was a Labor Day weekend, and the family was on the yacht in dock at Block Island. A terrifying storm struck suddenly and brought eighteen hours of gale force winds blowing at seventy miles per hour. There was real danger that they would lose the boat, but they stayed with it, kept the lines and bumpers in place, and they came through — the boat was not lost or even seriously damaged. Why did they stay with the boat? Not just because of the money value involved, though that was a considerable amount, but because they had so much of themselves invested in the boat.

The Preusses bought the boat in 1962. It is a forty-six foot, all-wood, classic boat built originally in 1930. The Preuss family worked on the boat for fourteen years before they finished their project of rebuilding and refurbishing it. They spent a lot of money on the job, but they also put a lot of themselves into it.

So when the boat was in jeopardy, they did not leave it to be battered against the dock and the other boats which were tied up beside it. They buffered the boat with tires and tended the lines hour after hour. When they finally decided they would have to get away from the dock to survive, they cast off and took their chances at getting out of the harbor into open waters. With good fortune they were able to steer through the tossing boats and get away to save their yacht. In the same way, Angela declares that perseverance instead of periodically seeking greener pastures has been a key to her success in business and in life.

Applying sound principles has been another key to her business success. Angela had only a high school education, so she had to build her success on the basis of one achievement built on the foundation of a level of achievement already reached. At each level of responsibility she mastered the job well, striving to be a super-achiever in that job. She worked hard at trying to win *every* contest and reach *every* goal in the company promotions. And she was willing to trust her ability to move up the management ladder and take on the responsibility of the next level in the company organization as opportunities opened or were created.

In her advance from personal sales to management, and then to an executive position, Angela found it crucially important to attract competent people to her organization, motivate them to high levels of achievement, and manage the organization to enable everybody in it to produce at their maximum capacity. Her philosophy was similar to that attributed to J. C. Penney: "Help your people succeed, and you can't help but be successful yourself."

On Becoming a Successful Person

When people learn the story of Angela's youth, and the struggles of her early adulthood, they often ask her, "Is it hard to live with success?" Her answer is, "No, not if you are a person who has some sense of authenticity about yourself." Her idea is that if you are an "all-together" person before you achieve success, then you will be an "all-together" person after you have experienced success.

Angela expresses a feeling that she, when she was a company vice-president, was not essentially different from what she was when she was a young woman working as an aide in a state mental hospital. There were differences in her job circumstances, to be sure, for in the hospital she was limited to an attendant's role in a little gray uniform, while in party-plan sales and management she had opportunity to use her mind and expand her career horizons. But, she insists, there was not a significant difference in her as a person.

For Angela, failure would have been hard to live with, but success would be hard to live with too if a person does not keep two feet on the ground. Success did bring some difficulties for her, however, primarily in the expectations other people had of her.

People who are less successful expect a person of wealth and position to be more of a super-person than they are. Angela found people expecting her to become more pretentious as she moved up the success and position ladder in the business world. She was not comfortable with those expectations.

The Preuss family has continued to live in the same house and the same neighborhood to which they moved in 1962 when their children were young and they were working to develop their businesses, he in equipment and she in sales. That tie with their earlier struggles and achievements gave an affirmation to the genuineness of their heritage and their accomplishments. They have indeed juggled life's pieces and put them together. Angela gives the impression of being a little "Janie" grown up, feeling very happy that she has pleased her mother by her achievements. She takes particular pride in having managed the roles of wife, mother, and businesswoman to succeed in all three.

Angela's Parents with Josie

Angela at Confirmation with godmother Katie Volpe

Angela at age 2

Rosie, Betty, and Angela

Angela and Carl's wedding

Carl and Angela at 25th Wedding Anniversary

Carl and Angela

Deborah

David

Angela at her desk

Donald

Her first mink coat

Her first company car

Angela doing a "Matter of Pride" demonstration

Angela with company founder at celebration of $1,000,000 level

Angela with her "Ten Million Dollar" goal chart

Angela with her family

Angela and Carl

65

Angela and Jo Nachman

Angela and her mother

*Angela, Gertrude Klein
and Carl*

Angela with her management team

Angela with Terry Lyden

Cleo and Helen Jeffers

Molly Lee

Pat Petrone

Angela with Joe Keenan and Corinne Marks

The Preuss Airplane

The Preuss Boat

Lennie Love

Callie Douglas receiving "Sweetheart of the Year" award from Angela

The Preuss Home

The Preuss Family Den

Carl's Store

Carl's Service Truck

Chapter V

Putting Punch in the Right Places

Motivating people is essential to effective marketing. It is doubly so with party-plan sales. Being a motivated person must come before one is able to motivate others, however, and that is how it has been with Angela. She learned early in her career of party-plan sales that she had to be a self-starter, and she had to be disciplined in her commitment to the job.

Punch to Propel Oneself

Initiative was cultivated in the Parisi children throughout their early lives, so a drive for success came easily to Angela. She readily recognized that she wanted to prove her self-worth, and she was willing to work for it. Her sense of being discriminated against as an immigrant Italian child stirred in her a desire to show others that she was just as good as they were.

Competition was a part of their lives even in childhood, for their father taught them to be competitive. Betty McDermott, Angela's younger sister, shared her memory of a family ritual which helped establish that drive. On Friday evenings when they were young their father would bring home five dollars in change. He would call the children together in the living room, pitch the coins into the air, and let the children scramble for them. What each one got was her pocket money for the week.

Early in life Angela developed a strong desire to achieve success, and she made a commitment when she was a young adult which reflects her personal determination to succeed. She said to herself over and over again, "I was born poor but I won't die poor." And she went to work on that goal, determined to reach it, so her dreams could come true.

71

Angela learned that to maintain a positive attitude helps keep you on the way toward your goal. A positive attitude tends to be self-actualizing, and it certainly proved to be so for her. The focus of her life was centered on her goal of success so completely that the possibility of failure was never able to cause negative doubts to trouble her. Her positive attitude toward success provided a propelling self-motivation which she used to the fullest.

Self-confidence was also a self-motivating personal characteristic for Angela. She cultivated her self-confidence by making sure she learned her job well and followed instructions carefully. When you know your job and prove to yourself by experience that you can handle it effectively, that expertise leads to self-confidence. Angela took advantage of the lessons and the opportunities of her early work experience to prove that she could perform with excellence and make a success of the things she tried to do. She discovered four sound principles of self-motivation which she applied very effectively in her own career.

1. Keep Busy At The Job. People who work in sales careers need to see sales grow in order to stay enthusiastic and highly motivated. For people in party-plan sales that means a full schedule of home shows since that is where their products are demonstrated and sold. Angela learned to keep her schedule of shows full by taking advantage of every home show to book other shows and to get recruit leads. She stayed busy, her sales grew steadily, and her increasing income motivated her to keep building her career and her sales organization even larger.

2. Work With Something You Can Be Proud Of. Confidence in the quality and value of the product you're selling increases your enthusiasm for marketing it. Early in her sales career Angela learned that valuable lesson by watching Connie Verin do a demonstration. Angela's sales were not even getting off the ground, while Connie was a top producer of sales. Angela attended one of Connie's shows and watched her in action. She observed that Connie loved the products she was showing, so she could describe them with glowing enthusiasm. She was proud of her products; she was highly motivated to demonstrate them attractively; and when she finished showing and describing her products the people bought them. Angela had learned from her one of the secrets of effective party-plan selling.

3. Put Some Creative Imagination Into Your Work. It's not enough to stay busy with a product you're proud of. You can do both of those things without being satisfied that you're really doing a super-achiever job. It's important also to apply your most creative imagination to planning how to do your shows. Settings, arrangements, displays, and suggestions for use are all part of successful home shows. Angela developed a technique which she called *romancing the products.* In her shows of home decor products, her approach was to cluster the products in related groups and present them in the most favorable settings. Atmosphere and lighting helped achieve the desired response of the guests to the products being demonstrated. When you love your products, and motivate others to fall in love with them, sales will follow. Creative imagination will help you have the kind of shows which cause people to really want the products you offer. You, your hostess, and her guests will enjoy such shows; and when your shows are enjoyable and profitable, there will be continuing strong motivation to book and hold more shows. This is the kind of incentive Angela used to cultivate hostesses for her shows and to keep herself busy at the job week after week.

4. Get In On All The Profit You Can. Angela's philosophy is to take advantage of every sales incentive that is offered. Party-plan sales companies make extensive use of contests, prizes, sales promotions, and personal achievement recognitions. These incentives are used to motivate sales representatives to book shows, do demonstrations, and make sales. They are an integral part of the party-plan sales method. Angela's attitude was one of driving determination to win every contest, even if the prize were only a pencil, and to meet every goal the company set forth. She recognized that these added incentives would increase the profitability of her work. Not only would she receive the additional value of any prizes she won, but in working for them she would increase her sales and receive the higher sales commissions which came with them.

Sales careers need to be profit-motivated. Angela's career was, and she used every additional incentive as a challenge to work after. She translated challenge into drive, and used it to keep herself motivated for her work and to keep her sales momentum going. Excellent sales and increasing income were the results. She turned opportunity into profit, and this in turn further enhanced the motivation of her personal drive for success.

Self-motivation is the foundation for a successful career in party-plan sales. Income depends on sales, and sales depend on consistent effective demonstration of your products at home shows. Success in personal sales led Angela into the field of recruiting and management, which brought her the additional new challenge of motivating others. She was successful by applying sound principles there also.

Punch to Propel Others: The Motivation of Caring

People learn to care by being cared about by others. Angela received deep and loving care as a child from her parents and from her godmother Katie Volpe. She learned early to care for others because of the handicap which her sister Rosie had. Rosie's deafness required special consideration from the family, and it exposed Angela to the students at Rosie's special school as she made weekly trips to accompany her back and forth. And being sensitive to people's feelings is a personal expression of care for them.

Respect for the human dignity of every person is another way to express care for people. Her experience of working in a state mental hospital provided Angela a good learning experience about human dignity. In the hospital the dignity of the patients and the lower level employees was not always treated with due consideration. Angela was wounded by some of the treatment she received while working there, so she vowed to always treat people with dignity and respect from the lowest menial level to the top executive officers.

Care and respect often lead to involvement in the lives and problems of others. As you demonstrate to people that you are on their side and want to help them, that expression will motivate them to try harder and believe in themselves more. Sometimes Angela spent time personally helping people in their development of business effectiveness. Sometimes she did personal things to help people who could not cope with personal problems.

Molly Lee was a regional manager in Angela's division. When she was beginning her work as a manager, Angela went to her home and spent several hours teaching her how to organize work schedules, manage correspondence effectively, and work "smarter" instead of merely working "harder." Some years later Molly wrote Angela a personal letter to express appreciation for the help and encouragement which had motivated her to keep trying. Molly wrote, "You made me feel so important by your interest and by taking time to teach me some of the tricks of the trade. You gave me confidence that I could manage my business."

Corinne Marks was creative and talented in party-plan sales. She was a top producer of sales in Angela's organization, but a time came when she needed professional therapy at the same time she needed to keep selling to supplement her family's income. Angela came to her rescue by making available the needed treatment. Corinne recovered, rebuilt her life and her business, and Angela's help played a vital part in motivating her to struggle out of depression to healthy and effective life again.

One of Angela's managers was Pat Petrone, a dynamic young woman. Her father was dying in Belgium and Pat could not borrow enough money commercially to make a trip there to visit him. Angela loaned her the necessary money which was later gratefully repaid.

Later Pat made a frantic phone call to Angela, "I can't manage any longer; I've got to have help." Angela went to see what could be done. She found the Petrone house in disarray and the family in chaos. For days Pat had been unable to cope with the demands of the house, their six children, and her job. So Angela took a cleaning lady and restored order to the house by working a long hard day on an icy February Saturday. She gave Pat a leave of absence for some recovery time. In the meantime Angela kept Pat's sales group together and functioning until she could take it over and manage the unit again. Angela's caring and help had proved vital to the recovery and motivation for effective business success by another of her people.

Angela's relationship with all the people in her organization was characterized by concern for them as persons and for their families. She tried to relate to the entire organization as an extended family. To cultivate this relationship Angela organized an annual family picnic for the people in her sales force. Getting acquainted with families, watching children grow up, and sharing concerns about illnesses strengthened the relationship between her and her people. Her care for them made them feel important and made them want to produce. Angela has lived by a philosophy that if "the company" has heart, then the company people will be happy to be a part of it, and they will be motivated to generate sales because of their loyalty and pride in "their" company.

The Punch of a Positive Approach

Negative attitudes tend to demotivate people. If you suggest that someone does not want to buy your product, you can be quite sure they will not want to. Many times such negative hints are not evident to a sales representative even when they are signaled quite clearly to a prospective customer. If on the other hand, however, you take a positive approach, you will find far more people responding positively and favorably to your sales or recruiting presentations.

One positive approach which Angela has used consistently is to focus on the good features of your product. She trained the people in her organization to present their party demonstrations with creative imagination to show their products in the most attractive settings. She also took the positive approach when recruiting workers and enlisting party hostesses. A sample approach was to call a person who had been suggested as a possible party hostess and say, "A friend of yours paid you a beautiful compliment last night. She said that you like lovely things." Such a beginning introduction tends to put a person at ease and create a favorable attitude which you can then capitalize on with your invitation to host a party and earn a lovely hostess gift by doing so.

Another positive aproach to be used in motivating people is to be sure you convince them that you are on their side and have their interests at heart. People are interested in hosting home shows for the gifts they receive, not for the commissions the demonstrator will make from the sales. Salespeople are interested in selling for the commissions they receive, not for the commissions their managers receive. So in booking shows you must demonstrate the benefits for the hostess, not for yourself. When you are recruiting people to sell, you must emphasize what they can earn in commissions and sales incentives. It is important for the people who work with you to sense that you get a lot of joy from their successes and from the good things which happen to them. Angela was always able to do this by emphasizing gifts and commissions to be earned, by offering bonuses for superior performance, and by showing enthusiasm for the accomplishments of her people.

To have confidence in people and to show it is a very positive way to motivate them. Confidence comes easily to Angela. When a group of people is gathered for a seminar, she approaches them with confidence that they can build a sales unit, reach a challenge goal, manage a business, and relate family and career effectively. From a beginning position of confidence, she proceeds to persuade them that they can do what is needed to accomplish the desired achievement.

Barbara Harrington worked as a regional manager in Angela's divisional organization. She has described one of Angela's strong features as the ability to recognize talents and develop them through confidence, training, and challenge. Angela will be satisfied with nothing less than a person's best. When she recognizes capability, she keeps reinforcing ambitious undertakings until that capability expresses itself in successful performance.

One of Angela's prime tools for motivating people is to demonstrate to them how they can affect their own paycheck by initiative and creativity. She operates out of a philosophy that super-achievers do not work *harder,* they work *smarter.* That approach is vitally important in party-plan sales, because different people achieve phenomenally different levels of success with the same line of products and in similar circumstances. Angela demonstrated the effectiveness of creativity by developing a plan to group her home decor products into categories and show them against a background which enhanced the beauty and usefulness of the individual items. She demonstrated initiative by preparing training materials for people in her unit when the company had no adequate training materials for such basic needs as how to book parties and how to demonstrate products.

Offering a quality product is also an important positive motivational factor. In the party-plan industry, companies which feature a high quality line of products also attract high quality people both as sales representatives and as customers. Such people are more easily motivated to be enthusiastic about a product and to be interested in that product. Since enthusiasm is motivating in itself, anything that contributes to enthusiasm also builds motivation. Selecting a high quality product to offer is a positive approach in recruiting people to work in sales and in persuading people to buy.

The Punch of Specific Actions

Motivation should always be intentional and planned. Sometimes, however, it should be forthright and direct, while at other times it should be more indirect and even subliminal. Angela has proved to be a master of both direct and indirect motivational approaches.

In a very open and direct way when working with persons and groups, Angela sets out intentionally to build a strong base of confidence in the product and the company being represented. Strong evidence to support the importance of such a base of confidence has often been reflected by people in Angela's organization. Lennie Love, a unit manager in the division, told Angela on one occasion, "We will sell if we are happy, but if we aren't happy with our company we just can't get it together." Specific planned actions are therefore indicated to acquaint people intimately and thoroughly with the products they are to offer and the company they are to represent.

Of equal importance is the motivation of people to have confidence in themselves. People need to feel sure that they can organize a product demonstration, book a home show, present a product, and manage sales and delivery arrangements. Motivators need to encourage development of such confidence by specific actions with persons and groups. Managers need to help make that confidence work through programs of effective training and continued support. The importance of self-confidence is readily evident because party-plan selling is so largely a self-starting kind of business for the individual salesperson.

An example of Angela's effectiveness in doing specific motivation with an individual is the story of Terry Lyden's success. She was born very poor. When she began selling the home decor products, she was living in a subsidized, low-rent apartment in a community of equally poor neighbors. Terri wanted to try, however, so Angela helped her book her first six parties and went with her to help her do her first show. That first party was held by one of Terri's neighbors, and it was evident that the environment was not really conducive to success. When they arrived, however, they found the friends had baked a cake and decorated it with "Good Luck, Terri." They were really trying to give her a good launching into her new venture. In spite of their encouragement, she had some rough days ahead. One day she came to a unit meeting with her feet so sore she could hardly walk. Angela asked about the trouble, and Terri reported that the day before she had knocked on forty doors without booking a single show.

Angela set about to help her develop the contagious enthusiasm which she needed for success. She suggested that Terri spend some time every day clapping her hands and saying to herself, "To be enthusiastic, act enthusiastic!" Two days later Terri called Angela to tell her that she had booked two parties, but now her *hands* were sore from having been clapped so much.

The following Christmas Terri thanked Angela for helping make it the best Christmas she had ever had, for she had been able to buy gifts for her family without charge accounts and months of after-Christmas bills. Terri Lyden went on to become a national sales winner in Angela's organization.

Another specific motivation Angela has used is to create a sense of personal investment and vested interest on the part of her people. She learned in her own life and in working with others that when a sense of pride is at stake a person is motivated to work doubly hard for success. This specific factor was used very notably in the year she led her division to undertake and exceed a sales goal of TEN MILLION DOLLARS.

Individual incentives are vitally important to personal motivation, and Angela majored on discovering those incentives and capitalizing on them. In one recruiting meeting a couple of retired persons were present. The husband was skeptical and asked a lot of questions. It turned out that he had reason to be distrustful, for he had been defrauded when he sold his dairy farm in preparation to retire. During the meeting Angela asked the group, "If you start selling with me, what will you do with the first five hundred dollars you earn?" The skeptical gentleman, Mr. Cleo Jeffers, answered, "Start me a solid bank account." He had identified his personal incentive and Angela picked up on it to do her recruiting with him.

Angela took a ten-dollar bill from her purse and said to Mr. Jeffers, "If you want a solid bank account, sign an application form, and then go open a savings account with this ten dollars so you'll have a place ready to put your earnings." He did it, and a couple of years later at a sales rally Cleo Jeffers showed Angela the evidence of his success. By that time Mrs. Jeffers had advanced to the level of a district unit manager. Mr. Jeffers showed Angela a bankbook with a substantial balance, and he pointed out to her the first entry. It was the ten dollars Angela had given him at the recruiting meeting.

Different incentives appeal to different people, so Angela has used a variety of incentives and rewards to motivate her people. Since 1962 the Preuss family has owned a yacht which was used for both family and business. Angela often rewarded top producers with complimentary weekends on the boat. Those weekends became memorable times in the lives of many people within her sales organization.

She also paid special attention to people who needed help to develop their own units within the division. Angela went to people to recruit and enlist them; then she had them come to her office at home for training. With Molly Lee, however, Angela did it differently. Molly was manager of a newly organized regional unit. Angela went to Molly's home and spent many hours helping her get organized and giving her some tips on how to make her work more efficient. She taught Molly how to manage mail so she would handle it only once, not two or three times. She shared with Molly some ways to add hours to her day by simply working more productively. Things Angela had learned by experience, and by trial and error, she gladly taught to other people in her company.

Success is a powerful motivator, and Angela proved it by encouraging Molly Lee to achieve success in party-plan sales. Molly went on to build a successful business which brought good profits to her and to the company. Later, when Angela left the company, Molly wrote to her, "You've been like a mother to me in my region. It's not so much what you do or say, but how you say it. We always use you as our example."

Recognition and rewards both play very important roles in providing specific incentives to motivate people. Early in her career as a manager Angela learned to use a communication network to share information and to recognize the accomplishments of individuals. With a typewriter and a mimeograph machine she began a newsletter which later became the *Preuss Press*. She reported the significant successes which different people achieved, and in doing so she gave them recognition which provided incentive to even greater future efforts and achievements. Success stories of those who were succeeding were also used to provide stimulus for the underproducers in the organization.

Angela made large use of recognitions at conventions to encourage people to strive hard to win contests and exceed outstanding sales goals. Built into the contests were attractive tangible gifts which people could earn and win. The party-plan industry recognizes the motivational encouragement of free trips to exciting places for conventions. Angela helped plan national conventions for the company in interesting places such as DisneyWorld, the

Bahamas, and Holland.

Not everyone can win the big prizes, however, so Angela developed ways to let people share vicariously in the joy of the success of others. Her division worked hard for eight years to develop a national queen in annual sales for the company. In the ninth year they finally had a national queen and continued on to win that honor for four of the next five years. One of Angela's secrets was to help all the people in her organization share the success of the winners. She played up the successes so everybody could get a thrill out of them. Angela tried to get all her people to dream of winning big prizes so they would work hard to reach high goals.

The Punch of Problem-Solving

When people are "down" they cannot produce like they can when they are "up." Discouragement and depressed feelings rob a person of the drive which is needed to pursue a goal effectively. Consequently anyone who is going to be self-motivated, and who can successfully motivate others must recognize the presence and negative effects of problems in life. The clue to dealing with problems effectively is to keep them from becoming a force for demotivation and turn them into a challenge for increased effort and achievement.

Angela met and overcame many problems in her own life. As she did she learned the importance of dealing positively with problems, and she learned by experience some ways to help others handle their problems to keep them from destroying their success. Her help to Corinne Marks and Pat Petrone, which reflected her personal care for people in her organization, also showed that she recognized how problems would hinder their work. She helped them get the problems out of the way so they could be successful again. Their personal successes brought business profits for themselves and for Angela.

A sales slump is always a critical problem for the people in the party-plan sales industry. Such slumps may be caused company-wide by economic recession or by bad decisions of management within the company itself. Slumps in individual sales may result from personal problems which reduce the number of parties held or the effectiveness of the demonstrator in showing the products.

Whatever the cause, it is imperative to take positive action to end the sales slump and get profits to rising again.

Angela knew that the first step in counteracting a sales slump is to restore the personal confidence of the sales people. Once, when her organization slipped into a slump and sales were falling behind projected goals, Angela dreamed up and used a campaign on the theme, "You're a Number One Person." She sent to each of her salespeople a small hand mirror with the campaign slogan printed on it. The central part of that confidence-building program was for each person to look into the mirror every day and say to herself over and over, "You're a Number One Person."

Another problem in party-plan sales is the danger of pitting people against one another in competition and hurting the losers. A key factor in motivating party-plan salespeople is the use of contests with attractive incentive prizes. Angela used such contests with real expertise, and she really encouraged her people to work hard for high sales in their efforts to win the prizes being offered. At the same time, however, she schooled her people to realize that in contests it is important to be prepared to lose as well as to win. Angela did two things to help ease the disappointment of those who did not win. She helped her people remember how much they had gained in increased commissions by their sales effort in the contest. So they really did not lose even though they did not win a specific contest prize. Angela also built into her organization a strong sense of shared joy for everyone in the successes of the whole organization and of the winners of special recognition. A philosophy of life which guided Angela in dealing with the problem of competition between people is that you do not have to put another person down in order to succeed yourself.

Summary

The key to effective motivation is to put punch in the right places. What are those places? Five are cruical.
1. One's personal need to be self-motivated.
2. The need of other persons to be cared about.
3. The need of people to be positively oriented.
4. The response of people to specific incentives.
5. The importance of turning problems into challenges

instead of letting them be stumbling blocks.

Angela demonstrated an innate insight into the motivational impact of these five factors. Her success as a manager of her organization was significantly enhanced by her skill at applying effective solutions to these motivational requirements.

Chapter VI

Meeting an Exciting Challenge

In 1978 Angela led her organization of two thousand people to reach a goal of TEN MILLION DOLLARS in sales in a single year. That was a goal which had never before been undertaken by anyone in Coppercraft Guild. The story of that year was a story of a challenge to accept, a campaign to organize, problems to overcome, motivation to maintain, and a final drive to direct.

A TEN MILLION DOLLAR YEAR came as the climax of nearly a quarter-century of hard work. For twenty-two years Angela had been busy recruiting, training, motivating, organization building, and strategy developing. She spent her first ten years in home decor product sales moving up from a beginning demonstator to a regional manager with one hundred seventy people in her organization. In 1967 Angela accepted a challenge to lead her regional unit to double its annual sales from half-a-million to a million dollars. They exceeded that goal. In ten years she had reached the first million-dollar level. By 1975 she had advanced to divisional vice-president of the company, and her division's sales were at the five-million dollar level. It was at that point she became aware of her need for a new challenge, so she dreamed a dream and fashioned a goal for herself and her division. She set out to lead her people to double their annual sales in three years and exceed the TEN MILLION DOLLAR mark in sales in 1978.

Angela's new dream had three facets. She wanted to enhance the image of the party-plan industry in the minds of people. She wanted to undertake something so spectacular that it would really excite all the people in her division at the thought of being a part of something so big. And she wanted to get into something more challenging than anything she had ever done before. She had already reached an income level which made her family com-

The Preuss Division Goal Chart
for the 1978 Ten Million Dollar Campaign

MONTH	%	SALES PROJECTED	SALES FOR THE MONTH	CUMULATIVE TOTAL SALES
JANUARY	5.1	$ 510,000	$ 338,894.30	$ 338,894.30
FEBRUARY	6.4	$ 640,000	$ 614,026.15	$ 952,920.45
MARCH	9.8	$ 980,000	$1,165,889.28	$ 2,118,809.73
APRIL	7.6	$ 760,000	$1,033,224.65	$ 3,152,034.38
MAY	6.2	$ 620,000	$ 707,480.48	$ 3,859,514.86
JUNE	7.2	$ 720,000	$ 722,110.32	$ 4,581,625.18
JULY	5.9	$ 590,000	$ 570,462.64	$ 5,152,087.82
AUGUST	7.4	$ 740,000	$ 615,751.42	$ 5,767,839.24
SEPTEMBER	10.6	$ 1,060,000	$1,488,627.64	$ 7,256,466.88
OCTOBER	12.8	$ 1,280,000	$ 919,174.63	$ 8,175,641.51
NOVEMBER	14.5	$ 1,450,000	$1,422,421.41	$ 9,598,062.92
DECEMBER	6.4	$ 640,000	$ 780,565.48	$10,378,628.40

fortably wealthy, so she planned to turn the added income from the campaign back into the campaign as incentives and rewards for the people of her division.

In the years 1976 and 1977 the division's progress stayed on track. Sales goals were met and the needed momentum was building. Angela had done her work well in goal development and in preparing her people for the challenge they were facing. Statistical analysis of previous sales experience indicated the exact percentages of annual sales which could be anticipated in each of the twelve months in the year. Angela programmed the division's monthly goals according to those percentages and charted their progress throughout the year by those goals. She was excited and enthusiastic as the challenge year of 1978 began. Then came the winter of 1978!

During that winter the northeastern and midwestern areas of the country where the Preuss Division was located were paralyzed by unusually severe weather. It was the worst winter of the century. Business plans and projected schedules were thrown completely off-track. By March the division was a half-million dollars behind its sales projections. The harsh winter and the accompanying sales slump took a terrific toll of discouragement from the people in the division. Angela knew that strong leadership from her was essential. Just as she had proved her skills at recruiting, training, and motivating; she now had to prove her effectiveness at problem-solving. She went to work.

Coming From Behind

First of all Angela organized a program of strong recovery actions. Knowing the importance of promotional public relations, Angela had asked for the support of company public relations resources but the company executives were not willing to give that support to her campaign. After the division fell behind in its sales, strong promotion was needed more than ever. Angela set out to do her own promotion.

She used her own divisional newsletter, the *Preuss Press,* to encourage her people to hold more parties and to work harder for sales to make up for their winter losses. The people's incomes, as well as the division's drive, needed a real boost in business as winter began to turn toward spring. Angela kept her people informed about their progress in relation to their goal. She promoted company incentives to the maximum. She worked doubly hard, using her reporting system for boosting efforts and encouraging the people throughout the organization. The initial recovery efforts helped, but they were not enough to get the campaign back on track.

In July Angela held a manager's improvement clinic. Her purpose was to get her unit managers back to a high level of enthusiasm and motivation. She took them back to the basics to get their perspective into focus again. The design was not to harass but to help, to get the organizational function back on track. Angela selected managers who were already performing with excellent success and used them to direct the clinic workshops. This highly motivated group of people communicated their enthusiasm and drive to the others, and the clinic proved to be a momentum-building event.

Then by October the pressure of time was upon them. Angela had two hundred fifty of her managers present at a divisional luncheon. Some of the people had not yet come out of their discouragement and losses of the previous winter. Angela talked with one manager that day who said she had only a single dollar in her pocket, but she was still unmotivated and discouraged instead of fired with determination to do something about it. Angela was struck with her plight, so she made an extra effort to spark enthusiasm for those present like her. She recapped all the resources available to them in the company's products, its programs, and its special incentives. The people had heard those things many times before, however, and still they were not using that knowledge to achieve successful results. Angela wondered why not. In her struggle to find an answer, she hit upon a word which became a theme word for the remainder of the campaign year. It was the word *PRIDE*, and Angela fashioned it into a campaign slogan "IT WILL BE A MATTER OF PRIDE — TEN MILLION." After the luncheon Angela furnished everybody a tee shirt with the slogan on it and they went home wearing them.

The people throughout the division responded. The idea of pride "hooked" their personal need for something to feel successful in doing. At last they went to work on the drive of the campaign the way Angela wanted them to do. Communication played a vital role in sustaining the momentum and building it even further. Campaign tee shirts announced their determination; they stamped it on all their business literature; they encouraged one another by keeping the slogan and the drive alive; they let the world know they were on their way to reaching their TEN MILLION DOLLAR goal.

Running the Home Stretch

One final thrust was designed by Angela to take the drive over its goal. She designated the last week of the year as "Loyalty Pride Week." Every salesperson was asked to send in one extra hundred dollar order that week with a "It's A Matter Of Pride" label attached to it. Contests were designed to get district groups to achieve one hundred percent participation in the loyalty week effort. Angela was primed to send from her division office a letter of thanks and a "Loyalty Pride" pin for every special order received.

That one-week drive brought in *Three Hundred Fifty Eight Thousand Dollars* in orders, and that was the largest single week of sales orders from any division in the history of the company. It was double the weekly average needed to reach their TEN MILLION annual sales goal. The Preuss Division had gone over the top — they had *EXCEEDED* their TEN MILLION DOLLAR goal! The final figure for the year was $10,378,628.40.

The Winner's Circle

Such an achievement called for a victory celebration. It was scheduled and held on January 27, 1979 at Leonard's of Great Neck, New York. At that moment Angela Preuss was sitting on top of the world. She had achieved phenomenal success and reached a level of financial reward and personal recognition for which she had dreamed, planned, and worked for twenty-three years.

Her success was shared by many others. Three hundred eighty five people bought tickets for the gala celebration and some of them traveled as much as twelve hundred miles to be there. A number of very special guests were invited. Included among them was the "father of the company" Earl T. Doty who unfortunately died ten days before the celebration was held. Angela's recruiter Gertrude Klein was present. One of her primary motivators was invited, Jim Pollard, who had recognized her potential and challenged her to become a regional manager and move her region to double sales and reach her first million-dollar level, but Jim also died before the date of the party.

The celebration dinner featured a sweepstakes drawing with an impressive array of gifts and a new car as a grand prize. Angela spent $20,000 for that evening as gifts for the people who had helped her reach the goal. Those gifts included a diamond gift for everyone attending as an expression of her appreciation for their support through the campaign. The managers of the division responded to show their esteem for their leader by presenting Angela a bracelet with her name set in diamonds.

Angela's mother was present to show her love and to share the joy of her very successful daughter. Carl and their children were there sharing in the well-earned recognition which Angela received, for the family had been a part of the many years of effort which came to culmination in that celebration.

The TEN MILLION DOLLAR year was a divisional effort and a divisional achievement. Angela provided the dream, the motivation, and the challenge. She set the pace, but the people in the division bought into the challenge and did the enormous amount of hard work required with enthusiasm and determination. That year brought success and profits to Angela, and many other people profited too. That highly successful campaign demonstrated Angela's conviction that a person cannot succeed without at the same time helping other people along the way toward success also. People throughout the Preuss Division profited from the commissions on the high sales they achieved during the campaign. The company profited from the record-breaking advance in sales which the division achieved during the drive to reach their goal. The exciting challenge of a TEN MILLION DOLLAR goal had motivated a lot of people to succeed during that campaign year. Hard work paid off generously. What a year it was for so many people!

Chapter VII

Complusions for Change

Angela was a young wife of twenty-five, with three pre-school children, when she began her career in home decor party-plan sales. Her need at that time was to supplement the earnings of her young husband who had just ventured into a new business enterprise. Additional income was needed to provide adequate family support.

That situation changed as Carl's business developed and prospered, and as Angela added one achievement to another in her sales career. She built her own business organization and moved up the company ladder from sales, to management, and then to a position of executive responsibility. The family became substantially wealthy, and their personal and family needs changed.

In fifteen years Angela had gone from a beginning sales representative to a company vice-president. She had proved her managerial and executive abilities. Two years after becoming a divisional vice-president she was asked to move "on track" and step into position to train and assume the presidency of the wascompany two years later. As Angela recalled that invitation a decade later she still remembered it as an overwhelming experience, one which she insists she will remember warmly when she is old and gray, because she was considered good enough in her professional field to be asked to become president of a major company.

She turned down the position, however, because it would have required relocation to the company headquarters and disruption of her husband's family business. Angela would not "put an apron" on her husband. She was not willing to exact that price from Carl for the opportunity of greater personal success for herself. A sequence of events was begun, however, which did later cause a career crisis and a career change for her.

Influential Motivations

At the mid-career point in her life Angela was faced with the question, "Where do I go from here?" The family was financially well-off. Angela had made significant achievements and lots of money. Carl's business was solid, and growing, so they had opened a branch store. They were out of debt. They owned a family yacht and an airplane. Carl and Angela's parental responsibilities and financial obligations for rearing their children were completed. So where should she go from there? Was retirement from business the way for her to go?

Without a strong challenge to motivate her any longer, Angela decided to retire. She bought a book by the title *Rehearse Before You Retire,* and spent two years trying to get herself ready for retirement. The more she tried to reorient her life to a retirement style, the more depressed she became. The outcome was a conviction that retirement was not for her. Angela Preuss had too much drive, too much ego energy, too much need to achieve success in the face of challenge to become a member of the social garden club set. She made a decision to put herself back into her business career with enthusiasm, to create new challenges for herself, and to find again the thrill of achievement. Her first mid-career crisis had been faced and resolved. Angela was still committed to her career as a businesswoman.

The year was 1975. From 1967 till 1975 she had led her sales organization to increase their annual sales from half-a-million to five million dollars. She had built her organization from region, to area, and to division; and with it she had been promoted from manager to vice-president. Having turned down an opportunity to become company president, where could she turn to design a meaningful challenge for herself. She decided that her area of challenge was in the area of outstanding sales achievements.

Angela was in her mid-forties. She had decided to focus her skills and her career efforts on additional sales successes, so she set out to write a new chapter for herself. A complete redecoration of her office became the first project. Then a new system of files and business plans were designed. While that was being done, she was working on the specific goal which she would use as her personal challenge. Her drive to excell was for her a compulsion for a change, the kind of change which achievement brings. So she identified for herself a new challenge in a campaign to lead her division to double their annual sales from five million to ten million dollars in three years. That goal provided her an absorbing three-year challenge which culminated in the phenomenal success of their TEN MILLION DOLLAR YEAR in 1978.

Three factors characterized Angela's motivational drive during those years of challenge and achievement. She had a *great solicitous interest in the people who made up her divisional sales organization.* Angela wanted very much to be the effective leader who would manage the operation of her division to provide the opportunities and incentives which would enable everyone of her people to be successful and prosperous in their own business units. She was highly motivated to be financially successful herself, but she was not selfish in her drive for success. She wanted others to achieve a lot of success also, believing that the success of every person in her division would mean success for them and for her at the same time.

The second motivational factor which characterized her drive was her *interest in the company.* Years before, as a beginning salesperson, Angela had fallen in love with the products she sold and the company she represented. She was firmly convinced that the products she offered were well worth their cost to her customers. She was also a strong believer in the way the company operated, providing good opportunities for income and prosperity to the people who worked in the company. Angela believed that if she made her division phenomenally successful the company would benefit by building its stature and increasing its profits. She applied her drive to succeed in a campaign which she intended to demonstrate a great love and steadfast loyalty to the company which had been so very good to her.

Angela was motivated by a third factor in her drive toward a TEN MILLION DOLLAR GOAL. Having turned down the opportunity to be groomed for the presidency of the company, she *needed a measure of achievement which would compensate her* for bypassing the offered promotion and *which would properly challenge her abilities* as she continued her business career. Angela was not emotionally suited to move along with undemanding and unexciting involvements. Her ego drive to achieve created compulsions for change and advancement. She constantly applied her imagination and her efforts toward satisfying her drive to achieve.

Corporate Conflict

Strong motivation brought signal success to Angela, but her drive also caused conflict between her and some other executives within the company. During the decade of the seventies, while Angela was in an executive capacity, the company was undergoing a great deal of corporate change. When she joined the company it was a young, family-owned enterprise. While Angela was in a managerial role the company was acquired by a parent company; and about the time she moved into an executive position, her company was acquired, along with its parent company, in a larger corporate merger. Those corporate changes affected the policies for operations and personnel within the sales organization which Angela had built and was managing.

The corporate management seemed to Angela to be more interested in company profits than in the well-being of their people. Benefits were changed and narrowed for the people in the sales organization, and Angela resisted those policy changes. Company management seemed to her to be insensitive to the problems and needs of people in the field. Angela always contended that attractive financial incentives for every unit of the sales organization were essential for the overall success of the marketing program of the company itself. The corporation executives did not always agree.

Executive change was also a part of the picture. The corporate changes of the seventies brought a rapid succession of presidential changes in the company. Evidently the executives who were elevated to the company presidency were threatened by the influence and drive which Angela demonstrated. Her long tenure and her executive position in the company, along with her strong influence in the division she had built, gave her more clout than the newly appointed presidents could comfortably deal with. She became convinced that they wanted her out of the company.

During the TEN MILLION DOLLAR YEAR of 1978, Angela tried to get the company president to lend his influence and use the public relations resources of the company to help her division achieve its goal. He was not willing to help. His response was that the campaign was too self-oriented. He seemed to fear that success in that campaign would strengthen the "Angela cult" nature of her division and further expand her influence within the company.

By the end of 1979 corporate decisions were made to reorganize

94

the company structure and eliminate the divisional vice-presidency office which Angela held. The executive management of the company apparently did not want one person to earn as much money or wield as much influence as Angela did. So on December 17, 1979, Angela was called to the home office of the company and informed that her position with the company was terminated. A uniquely successful career in the party-plan sales industry was ended.

A Second Mid-Career Crisis

While Angela had been aware of policy conflicts between herself and some other company executives for several years, and although she was sure some of them wanted her out of the company, her termination was nevertheless a shocking surprise to her. It was done with devastating suddenness, and it caused deep grief to her, especially so since it came at the otherwise joyous season of Christmas. Waves of shock were felt throughout the company, but most keenly within the Preuss Division. The people she had recruited, trained, motivated, and led throughout their whole careers with the company had had their leader removed from her place at the head of their organization. Change for Angela would also mean radical change for them, emotionally if not in other ways. Things would no longer be the same in the Preuss Division of the company. Angela's presence, her spirit, and her drive would not be there.

WHAT HER PEOPLE SAID! Angela's influence on the people of her division and throughout the larger company was reflected in their response to her removal from her executive position. Their first expressions of shock and grief were to her. Telephone calls, visits, and letters poured in, expessing both sadness and outrage.

Some of the people wrote about *the personal things Angela had done for them.* Her way of relating to people was to get personally involved with them in their business and to be sensitive to their personal and family joys and problems.

Charlotte Madar wrote:

I have always appreciated all the help and inspiration you always gave to me so willingly and unselfishly. And how very much I admire your talents, accomplishments and your thoughtfulness. I still have the note you sent me when my son Geoffrey was born.

Karen Treonze wrote:

Even as a counselor you always made me feel so important to our group just by saying, "Hi, Karen." I felt so terrific to have someone as special as you call me by my first name.

Bonnie Nelson wrote:

Never in my life have I ever been so proud or ever felt so fortunate as when I was associated with you. I'll never be able to, or ever want to, forget the things you've taught me. Because they weren't parts of business but parts of life . . . I'll succeed, I know I will; but most of all because of you. You gave me a goal — a lifetime goal! . . . I want to be as great as you are because honestly, half isn't good enough! Not for someone like me who has been inspired by the best!

And Molly Lee wrote:

It is almost frightening when I think about that time when I couldn't cope and I came to you for help. Little did I know that you wouldn't be there forever . . . You were so good to me, you took time from your super-busy schedule and came to my humble home to help little ole me . . . I felt honored . . . because of your willingness to help and the joy you got out of assisting us. Your eagerness to do anything you could to help us help ourselves . . . made us feel so important when we felt so insignificant.

Some others of the people *wrote about the ways Angela had motivated them,* and how she had used incentives to encourage them, to help them become successful party-plan people and achieve the successes they had dreamed of.

Nancy Wazak wrote:

A watch . . . diamonds . . . gold . . . and now a fox — gorgeous gifts I will always treasure from a "truly special" person. But I really think the gift I will treasure most is the gift of yourself that you have been giving for over 5 years I have known you, Angela. You have shown me that special gift of "caring" that most people only talk about.

Trudy Bonica wrote:

Angela, I confessed to you once (at the Cape Cod convention) that certain things motivate me to succeed — trips, money, etc. — but I still have you on my list. I think about you often — you — a successful person who gave it all and persevered.

Carolyn Tubbs wrote:

Thank you for all the gifts you gave me and the most special gift you gave me is the gift of your *time!* The *times* of teaching — the *times* of fun — the *times* of yourself giving and sharing with me.

Jo Ann Hemm wrote:

No one has been more of an inspiration in my life than you. The 1st time I heard you I wanted to get up and go and sell — that very minute.

Synnore Andresean wrote:

You're a self made person, a superstar among the greatest stars and your teachings will shine on many lives for the rest of their lives for what you *gave away!* You taught me to set my priorities... Now Angela, you see the difference, I have no doubt I'll get it! That's your training! I believe it! and I'll get it!... With what you've taught me, the motivation which you have inspired within me, and my own initiative, I can't help but come out a winner! Wow!! I'm only one person — do you realize what you've given to thousands?... You have the power to bring out the best in anyone.

And Shirley Goodfleisch wrote:

You are a woman of tremendous vitality and energy which no one can suppress — and I feel sure that very soon you will channel this energy into something worthy of Angela Preuss.

Many of the letters Angela received after leaving the company referred to *the influence of her teaching and training.* People who worked with her were aware of the great help her early preparation and continued guidance had been to them. Angela herself had been helped in that way by her own White Cross recruiter Gertrude Klein. The lessons she learned from Mrs. Klein helped her get started well. Throughout her management career Angela gave special attention to training her people thoroughly in the basics and in the finer points of group selling through home shows.

Karen Orstrander wrote:

Thank you so much for caring about... the people within the company to make them stronger leaders and develop their attributes. I want you to know that I really appreciate the time you spent putting me on the right track.

Regina Hampton wrote:

Your purpose was to touch hearts and bring confidence to people all over the country.... I can say this because I know the entire Love District was touched by the magic word of "Mother Preuss." . . . You will always be our leader and guiding force.

Dodie Rayman wrote:

I want to thank you . . . for all the training and sharing that was done in the five years I was with you. I really feel like I have learned a fantastic amount, and I'm sure that my future success will be due to the beautiful people who have shared their lives and training with me. You are unbelievable, and I will never forget you. I'll keep you posted on how I'm doing so you can see how well I've learned from you.

And Carolyn Tubbs wrote about the training Angela had given, as well as the way she had given of herself to her people:

I treasure everything you taught me (about business and personal) . . . I always said you are a special person who is always to *lead* and *teach* as God has chosen you to do that.

Angela has always been conscious of how important it is for a career woman to balance *her roles as person, wife, mother and businesswoman.* Her concern to relate those roles to one another in a healthy way caused many of her people to be influenced by her in that area.

Nancy Jones wrote:

You have been a symbol of hope to many of us that are working hard to succeed at our roles as wives and mothers as well as career persons.

And Donna Keife wrote:

I sincerely hope you and Carl have a long and happy life together. With the love you two share I know that won't be difficult to do.

The grief her people experienced at her leaving the company was expressed in their *apprehension about the future.* All the people in the Preuss Division had worked under Angela's management throughout their careers with the company, most of them throughout their entire experience in party-plan sales. Now she would no longer be at their head as leader and motivator. A new situation would exist for them as well as for her, and for many of them the prospects were alarming.

But mostly, even the letters to the company officers told about Angela and *the helpful influence she had been* for the people in her division. For instance, Diane Toto also wrote:

Angela is like a tiny acorn who, after 23 years, grew into a mighty oak ... Angela possesses the rare gift of good business sense and deep concern for her people. Angela always said (the company) is a people business. It's a family, and families have to stick together ... Her inspiration and unshakeable faith in (the company) and in people made me and others do seemingly impossible things.

Ann Danziger also wrote about *the encouragement Angela provided* her when she was moving into the new area of securing orders from restaurants and other businesses. She described an order for $495 she got because Angela loaned her some sample products to leave with prospects and carefully coached her step-by-step in what to say and how to close the sale. She wrote:

I don't know how many times I just "fell in" on her. Once I told Angela she would throw me out some day. Her answer was, "That's what I'm here for ... to help you." THAT'S WHAT YOU FIRE?!

Sandra Firestone wrote:

Angela has been our inspiration, our motivator and our mentor. She had molded ordinary housewives into business people. She has given of herself and her time, and shared her family and her home with us. She has been with us through success and failure, through joy and sadness ... You have broken our spirits and destroyed our dreams, shattered our hearts and made us afraid for the future ... Give us back our leader, Angela Preuss.

Donna Keefe wrote:

It seems impossible that you won't be at our rallies, bingos, etc. to add the class and grace we need.

Dot Wazak wrote:

I feel badly that there will be no luncheon tomorrow, that you won't hear me talk at the workshop, that there won't be prompter pride luncheons — about all the things that "won't be" anymore. But I am very proud to have worked for you, to have been invited into your home, to have learned from you, to have shared your special celebration, to have gotten to know you in a personal way, to have been your chaffeur and a lot more ... I can only say that I am happy that our lives have touched.

And Marie Wood wrote:

My sadness comes with the thought of losing your friendship and guidance. I will always treasure the six years I have spent as part of the Preuss Division.

Letters went *to the executive officers* of the company. Some of them described *the difference Angela's termination made* in their feeling about the company.

Ann Danziger wrote:

> I have been with (this company) for five years, and until a year ago I DID believe in (it). I'm afraid I don't anymore.

Diane Toto wrote:

> We're no longer part of a family, we're just cogs in a machine. Without motivational help from Angela there won't be as many achievers becoming superachievers, and in the long run I feel (the company) and their sales will be the losers.

And Cathy Perotta wrote:

> This lady is *not* a "word person" . . . she is an action person . . . Angela Preuss is a people person who cares and gives of herself.

All the expressions of sympathy and support, of shock and outrage did not change the situation, however, for Angela had been fired and that action was not being reconsidered. Another severe career crisis had come for her.

CAREER CRISIS OF A DIFFERENT KIND! Years before, Angela had been dismissed from an earlier job. As a teen-ager she had been fired from an ice-cream parlor job because she tried so hard to succeed that she would not listen to the instructions her employer gave her. That incident was short-lived and proved to be a helpful lesson. Angela went back the next day, told her boss she had learned that she must follow instructions, and she was given back her job.

Now in mid-career she had been fired again for being so dedicated to people-centered sales principles that she wouldn't give in to profit-centered executives in the company. This time she wouldn't get her job back, so she had to deal with a second mid-career crisis.

Angela's first crisis a mid-career came from super-success. It seemed that she had reached all her challenging goals and retirement time had come. As Angela discovered, however, retirement was not for her. So she set some new goals for herself and started work on a challenge which led her to new heights of success in a TEN MILLION DOLLAR sales year. Her second crisis at mid-career, however, was a crisis of a different kind, coming in the apparent failure of being fired from her executive position. How would she handle that crisis?

Severing her business associations with the people of her former division was very painful for Angela. She no longer had her people to lead. She no longer had the challenge to set high goals and work hard to devise successful programs which would achieve them. Her career had been a large and vital part of her life for twenty-one years and ten months. It had been suddenly taken from her. Her compulsion for challenge and change, which she had fashioned into a drive to move upward and achieve ever-higher goals, had resulted in two things. Her drive had caused her to outgrow any place the company had to accomodate her ambition. Her drive had catapulted her upward in the company and at last out of the company and the career which she loved. She was now unemployed at age forty-eight.

Where would Angela go to invest the rest of her life, to employ her drive, satisfy her ego, use her skills, achieve her still enthusiastic ambitions, and fulfill her dreams. Her compulsion for challenge and change, and her drive to achieve, were so great that she would not accept a condition of forced unemployment. Angela Preuss would turn apparent defeat into a new direction of achievement.

VIII

Dreams With Handles

Through the experiences of life, flashes of insight became a part of Angela's way of seeing things. Those insights became the roots of her later career dreams.

Her first job as a child was harvesting potatoes for a "per bushel" rate. She learned quickly that volume of business is a key factor in success and income. In her ice cream parlor job she was convinced that if they gave large cones of cream for the money then lots of people would want to buy from them. She was sure that good value for the price would attract a large volume of business. She had to learn from her boss that sales have to be profitable to the company as well as good values for the customers. During her work in the mental hospital she experienced abusive treatment which convinced her that personal values and human dignity are vitally important in business relationships and wherever people are involved with one another.

Angela got into party-plan selling because she wanted the kind of work that would let her stay home with their baby while Carl was away during the day at his job. Once into party-plan selling she discovered that group selling in people's homes creates a situation where volume sales are possible with low overhead costs. That in turn makes it possible to offer good value products at attractive prices and still make attractive profits. The pieces of her business philosophy were beginning to come together.

Care about people, offer attractive products at good value prices, and work hard after volume sales; these were the basic principles on which Angela Preuss built her success as demonstrator, manager, and executive in a party-plan sales company. Through more than two decades in home decor party-plan sales she fashioned those principles into dreams about a company, dreams about an enthusiastic sales force, dreams about a line of beautiful and substantial products, and dreams about a sales program which encourages super-achievements by creative people. What she saw as shortcomings in company programs within the party-plan industry became her dreams about what a company should avoid as it fashioned an ideal program for both company and people.

Dreams About A Company

Angela described her philosophy of a successful company in a training lecture which used a tree for comparsion. She described a company as being like the trunk of a tree which must be solid and provide strength, support, and security for the people associated with it by furnishing products, programs, and organization which will be motivating incentives for success.

A company, like a tree, must have a healthy root system firmly rooted in fertile soil for good growth to take place. The root system for a company is found in the executive leadership, the owners, the financial base, and the business philosophy which is translated into company policies.

And it is on the branches that a tree produces fruit. So it is also with a company. In the party-plan sales industry, the individuals who hold shows, demonstrate products, and make sales are the key producers of the success of the company. It is essential therefore, that a company have the loyalty and dedication of its people in order to be successful on a continuing basis. An effective company is one which combines product, program and people in a successful combination, so like a tree it has roots, trunk, and branches.

Angela's business philosophy is built upon a conviction that a high quality product-line is basic, for products which have quality and value attract people who have awareness and appreciation for things of quality and value. So if you want your business to be successful, start with a product-line which high quality people will appreciate and want, for products which attract customers will also attract people to demonstrate and sell them, and salespeople who have high personal goals are people who are easy to motivate. Just offer incentives for achievement, and people with high aspirations will motivate themselves.

So Angela dreamed of a company whose approach would be too offer attractive products at affordable prices, attract highly motivated people to work for the company, and provide incentives for super-achievement. She was disappointed when the company she worked for seemed to be hampering her growth and putting a lid on her expansion. She was convinced that by helping every demonstrator be successful, and by developing more and larger regions within her division, she could contribute to the increasing success and profitability of the company if it were all managed efficiently in the production and supply areas as well as in sales. Her dream was of a company which would be like a tree, with deep roots and a strong trunk supporting a system of growing branches producing lots of fruit.

Dreams About People

Angela proved that she was a super-salesperson. She recruited, trained, motivated, and managed a sales organization which constantly added new people, opened new markets, expanded into new areas, and increased sales to ever-higher levels. She did it by believing in people and cultivating their enthusiasm.

Showing respect for personal dignity and providing incentives to excel were two key features of her successful motivation philosophy. Angela convinced the people she recruited and trained to believe in themselves, in their product, in their company, and in their ability to sell. As a consequence they became successful in their work, and as a result they believed in Angela as their leader.

A sales force of highly motivated, enthusiastic, and well-trained people was one of her dreams, so Angela worked hard and creatively to develop such a sales force. She succeeded admirably. Whenever company policies created disincentives which reduced enthusiasm, Angela always worked to try to change those policies.

So Angela's dreams included both a company and its people. Her dream was of a company which would help people to dream and which would bring out the best in them as they worked to make their dreams come true. Her dreams of the company's people were that they should be highly motivated by positive attitudes and ambitious aspirations to be successful and happy people in their work and in their homes. Caring about people was a continuing source of her beautiful dreams for them.

Dreams About Incentives to Achievement

Products and programs are vital parts of business success. A successful product is one which people want, and which can be offered to them at a price that makes it a good value to buy. Successful programs are ways to encourage sales which are profitable to the company and to the seller while pleasing the buyer with the quality and the value of the product.

A company which has a good product also needs a good sales program to market that product and reward the sales representative. Efficient training and motivation, therefore, are essential parts of a company sales program, for getting people ready to sell is a key factor in their successful effectiveness in sales work.

Angela's dreams about incentives were that every person in her organization would have the motivation of self-confidence, the motivation of enthusiasm, the motivation of attractive profits to be earned, and the motivation of special bonus rewards to be won. She believed that if the company offered the training to develop self-confidence and enthusiasm, and if they offered the incentives of commissions and bonuses, then the people would produce volume sales and both would profit. If a company helps its people succeed, they in turn will want to help the company be profitable for their own future success will be made secure by it.

So Angela dreamed dreams. Some of them came true in striking ways because of the hard work and creative efforts she and her people applied to their personal and organizational goals. But some of her dreams were thwarted because of a different business philosophy held by other executives in the company. She was oriented towards sales. That was her specialty and she was effective at it. Those who were responsible for production and inventory did not always agree with the way the sales force in the field wanted things to be done. Consequently, both fabulous achievements and frustrating conflicts were part of Angela's last years with the company which had afforded her success and wealth. For some of her dreams she could not find handles to accomplish. Then a shattering of dreams broke upon her through dismissal from her executive position. Angela was quite a bit like Dorothy in the Land of Oz when in the Emerald City she learned that there was no Good Wizard who could make her dreams come true. Personal dreams and career dreams were in limbo as she set about to find a new direction and fashion a new challenge for herself. She had to learn that the wizard was make believe. Like the Scarecrow who wanted brains, the Tin Woodman who wanted a heart, and the Cowardly Lion who wanted courage, Angela had to make herself believe that, if she would only believe, she could have the answers to her dreams.

So where would Angela go? Into a business of her own? She had already learned that she was not emotionally suited to a retirement style of life so early in life. That option was laid aside quickly. Was she ready to go back into a job where someone else made the executive decisions? And could she find such a job? Opportunities of that kind came quickly and attractively. Her sales and motivational skills were in ready demand, but Angela decided against a salaried job. A business of her own — could she really pull it off?

A New Venture: New Handles for Her Dreams

Angela and two past presidents of her former company, Joe Keenan and Jim Pfleider, learned of a small party-plan company dealing in boutique sales of fashion accessories which was being offered for sale. It was a young company, at that time only four years old. It was a small company, owned and managed by Don and JoAnn Swensen, and operating in a limited area of the Midwest. But Angela, Joe, and Jim were quite impressed with its potential. They decided to form a partnership and buy the company. They did, and relocated its headquarters to Minneapolis, Minnesota. Their dream and plan was to develop their new company into one of the best party-plan companies in America. Thus Angela entered the new venture of partnership in *Passeport Boutique.*

The company entered a new chapter in its history with the advantage of experienced leadership. Between them the three owners had seventy-three years of experience in business and party-plan sales. The former owners, the Swensens, stayed with the company as salaried vice-presidents and added another twenty years of party-plan experience to the new company's leadership. So Passeport Boutique began with leaders who were professionals in their field. They had already learned through their years of experience the kinds of programs that will work and those that won't. Their expertise gave Passeport Boutique a flying start which made for rapid development by the young company.

Angela's role in the new company was to be the field executive to develop and manage the sales forces and the sales programs. Her dreams, fashioned in past years of super-achievement, now had a new handle. In the new company she could let her great creative ambition begin to develop the kind of sales organization she had longed for.

Her role, however, would no longer be exclusively in sales. Joe Keenan described her entry into Passeport Boutique as one which would involve her to a greater extent in executive management. As one who had worked with her in home decor product sales and now had joined her in an executive partnership, he observed that she made the transition easily and effectively to part-owner and field president.

Angela and her partners went to work to build their company into an enterprise which would meet the expectations and fulfill the aspirations which had motivated them to undertake this daring new venture, investing large amounts of their personal money and large segments of their personal efforts.

Company Philosopy: Three Central Features

Passeport Boutique is not just another party-plan company. It is a product of a conviction that a successful business is built on three primary foundations: opportunity, people, and leadership. A business philosophy focused on the inter-relation of those primary factors was planned into the company from its acquisition by the new owners, who went into the venture with a commitment to be the best.

UNLIMITED OPPORTUNITY. Angela brought to Passeport Boutique her commitment to work with personal pride to make it a company which provides great potential for profit and success to everybody associated with it. The opportunity offered by Passeport Boutique is based on quality products offered at affordable prices, and sales programs which are designed to provide attractive profits to sales representatives and to the company at the same time.

Joe Keenan has analyzed this philosophy from two points of view, the company and the sales representatives. From the company point of view, profitability success depends upon sales leadership and organization in the style and character of Angela Preuss' mode of operation. From the point of view of sales representatives, the company must be a *people developing enterprise.* People without special skills or sales experience are provided training and motivation which enable them to become effective and prosperous business people. People in the company are offered opportunity and encouragement to develop self-confidence and active interests in creative accomplishments.

Angela's goal is to help Passeport Boutique coordinators and directors be among the highest paid people in every community. In order to reach that goal is her intention to provide to every Passeport representative the encouragement and help needed to achieve their top potential. No restrictions will be placed on individual growth, for the success of the people will insure the success of the company. Passeport Boutique must be proud of it and satisfied to be a part of it. She is convinced it must be that kind of company for the company people to be proud of it and of her as their leader.

A COMPANY WITH HEART. The second feature of the Passeport Boutique business philosophy is based on the conviction that the most important thing in the world is people. They are to be loved and helped, not used. They are to be motivated and encouraged, not abused. They are to be respected and valued, whether their sales are large or small.

Joe Keenan describes the people-orientation of the company as such that it in turn can become a part of their lives. The company's relation to people is oriented to motivation and encouragement, being perceptive to people's interests, and offering interest-oriented products.

Angela brought to Passeport Boutique a career-long commitment to a people-oriented approach to business and to life. Because of this emphasis on people, the approach of the company is designed to be positive and constructive in programs of training and marketing. Negatives demotivate, so the Passeport company is committed to avoid negatives, or to eliminate them.

Care for the feelings of people means that in the Passeport organization people will not be played up against one another. Promotional programs are so structured that achievement is recognized, and super-achievements are admired and praised; but contests and promotions are designed so *everybody can be a winner* at some level. Everyone is thus encouraged to feel that they can measure up and achieve a worthwhile goal for oneself and for the company. No person's success should be at the expense of others, so everyone can be happy for the highest achiever and for themselves in their own achievements.

Angela works hard to keep heart in the company, as well as sound business management. Good business does not mean that human dignity must be sacrificed. Nor does preserving human dignity mean that company profits are of no concern. Management with heart means that you treat people with careful concern for personal dignity, even as you work with them for the profitable benefit of the company. Working with people means that you help them perform well in the company if they fit well there, or find a way to move out of the company happily to something more fitting to their abilities and interests. Whether people are being helped to become super-achievers, or being helped to find their way out of the company. Passeport Boutique is committed to deal with them in a caring way. Passeport is committed to be a company with heart.

QUALITY LEADERSHIP. The standards of quality for a company are set by the leaders of that company. They have the influence, and they need to have outstanding personal qualities themselves. High ideals, integrity, fairness, competence, and respect for people are vital qualities for a leader who will help build a quality company.

"Water seeks its own level" is an easily demonstrated truism. Likewise, a quality company attracts quality people. *Quality leadership* will develop a *quality company* by choosing to deal in *quality products* and by designing *quality company policies,* which in turn will attract *quality people to represent* the company and *quality customers to buy* the company's good quality products.

An Italian adage from Angela's heritage goes, "a fish stinks from the head." Applied to business that adage means that when a company goes bad it is due to failure on the part of responsible leaders to give sound leadership to the company. By contrast, effective leaders will develop good programs, enlist and motivate capable people, and generate contagious enthusiasm throughout the life of the company.

Negative-thinking people say, "It can't be done." Positive-thinking people say, "The difficult we do immediately; the impossible takes a little longer"; for positive-thinking people believe that seemingly impossible things can be accomplished. Good leaders are positive-thinking people whose focus is forward and whose perspective is progressive.

Intelligent hard work is far more productive than mere hard work. Quality leadership knows the difference. By insight or experience, leaders learn to identify ways to do intelligent and creative hard work. Angela and her executive partners in Passeport Boutique had already learned programs that will work and programs that won't work before they embarked on the venture of acquiring the Passeport company. They had already developed and proven their ability to provide skilled and competent leadership in how to work intelligently and how to sell successfully. Passeport Boutique's quality leadership enabled the company to develop on solid ground and build rapidly into a progressive and profitable enterprise.

Company Organization: Four Sound Principles

Based on their experience and insight, the executives of Passeport Boutique established their company on four sound principles for making a party-plan company attractive and successful. These principles are profitably applicable to other marketing approaches as well as to group sales through home shows.

OFFER QUALITY PRODUCTS. Angela's sales philosophy is based on the principle of offering for sale products which are attractive and have wide appeal. When such products are offered at prices which are affordable to large numbers of people, then volume sales can be achieved. Repeat sales are also a significant factor in determining the continued volume and profitability of a company's sales. Repeat sales can result from offering seasonal products, marketing expendable products, or adding new products to the company's line.

Angela and her partners chose fashion jewelry as the line for the new company they would build. This product-line met the tests of her sales philosophy. Fashion jewelry is specifically designed to be attractive and it has wide appeal among both men and women. Lovely fashion jewelry is available at Passeport Boutique shows at quite affordable prices, so almost anyone who attends a Passeport Boutique party can buy one or more pieces which will go beautifully with clothes they already have or plan to buy.

Since clothing styles change with the changing seasons, and since gift giving is both perennial and holiday oriented, repeat sales of fashion jewelry are a prime source of volume sales for Passeport representatives. Changing styles and continuous product design also enables Passeport Boutique to add new items to its jewelry inventory regularly. Angela and her company have established a product-line which offers an open opportunity to apply her sales philosophy creatively.

INVOLVE CAPABLE PERSONNEL. The second factor involved a successful sales organization in its personnel. Angela learned early in her management career that constant recruiting and effective training are essential to getting and keeping people who are capable of becoming high achievers. A company must offer challenge if it hopes to attract people who have ambition, and ambition and enthusiasm are necessary ingredients of successful sales work. Successful recruiters must be constantly seeking for people who "fill the bill", and they must be positively optimistic as they try to interest potential recruits in the company and its products. Then when people have been recruited to become sales representatives, it is essential that they be adequately trained to market the products of the company through the sales programs of the company.

Good training accomplished good things for both the company and its personnel. Angela experienced personally the difference between good training and the absence of good training in the beginning of her own sales career. When Gertrude Klein recruited Angela for her first sales work with the White Cross Home Products Company, she coached her carefully in the way to market those products well. By contrast, when Gertrude Daniels recruited her to work with Coppercraft Guild, she simply delivered the kit of sample products and left Angela to find her own way. Apparently she assumed that because Angela had been a high producer for White Cross she could do the same again without any need for help. Consequently Angela floundered along with disappointing results and was almost discouraged enough to quit. Finally Mrs. Daniels suggested that Angela go to a showing with an effective, experienced demonstrator to observe and learn some clues about how to do effective home-decor products shows.

After Angela became a unit manager, she developed training materials for her people, and paid a lot of attention to training new people and continually upgrading the skills of all her people. She has maintained her commitment to effective training throughout her career as a business executive. For good training enables capable people to become successful, and successful people make happy and profitable representatives for a company. Good training, therefore, is beneficial to a company because it reduces personnel turnover rates and it improves the profitable productivity of the company's personnel. And good training is beneficial to individual sales representatives for it enables them to have good feelings of competence and confident feelings of success.

And regular communication with her people has been a significant part of Angela's training and motivation approach. She has made very effective use of unit newsletters at every level of her managerial and executive career. Through her newsletter she keeps her people informed about the latest product developments, sales techniques, company programs, and bonus incentives. She seeks to insure that her people know their products and the best ways to market them.

DEVELOP HIGH INCENTIVE PROGRAMS WHICH MOTIVATE. Quality products and capable people are essential, but a company needs an effective sales program if its marketing process is to work. Company managers know that they must have a program which provides opportunity, encouragement, and incentive for its sales representatives. Achievement must be profitable, or there will be no adequate incentive to strive after higher achievement.

Angela is oriented to profitable incentives for high achievement. She learned in the potato fields as a teen-ager that if you fill a lot of baskets your pay will increase if you are being paid a unit price for each basket. In party-plan sales she learned that you can determine your own paycheck by the sales you make.

In her career as a unit manager and as a company executive she has worked to develop programs which encourage her people to try to reach high goals because high rewards come with them. Challenge goals, special promotions, and incentive bonuses provide motivational features of the sales programs Angela has used and developed through the years.

Effective sales programs must avoid features which tend to demotivate people. Through the years Angela has believed that three things often found in company programs tend to have an adverse effect on party-plan sales. They are: programs which require the customer to place an order and wait for the delivery of the merchandise, programs which require company representatives and hostesses to package and deliver merchandise which has been ordered, and programs which require those who sell to wait a period of time to receive commissions on their sales.

Passeport Boutique has a sales program designed to avoid those three demotivating features. Passeport sales representatives maintain their own inventory of products, so at boutique showings they sell items which the customers carry away with them at that time. The transaction is completed, so the customer has the product and the seller has profit in-hand immediately. This sales and delivery process, is more pleasing to the customer, to the party hostess, and to the seller. This approach also allows the company to operate with reduced costs so products can be attractively priced and additional profit incentives are possible for the sales representatives.

Angela has a multi-faceted sales program which is designed to motivate her people to expand their own sales activities and to recruit other people to join the company as sales representatives. The base line is a high profit percentage on sales. To that can be added continuing recruiting fees which are available to all sales representatives as well as to unit managers. Attractive periodic contest prizes are an additional incentive open to all Passeport personnel. Monthly cash bonuses for sales exceeding established levels add profits for even moderate producers. In the area of management incentives, Passeport Boutique pays high over-ride commissions on unit sales, director incentive fees, and spin-off fees through the Management Earning Program which rewards people for helping the company sales organization to grow.

The "name of the game" is profits. Angela is committed to help her people earn attractive incomes and enjoy the benefits of financial affluence. For that reason she strives to provide the program, the training, and the incentives which will enable every representative in her sales organization to advance as high as their individual abilities and willingness to work can carry them.

ESTABLISH EXCELLENT COMPANY STANDARDS.

The first three principles for building an attractive and profitable company will succeed only if the company itself, through its executive leadership, is committed to high standards of professional and personal performance.

High ideals are contagious. Company executives set the tone for attitudes and performance within the company. Positive-thinking, progressive, enthusiastic company leaders will help those same qualities prevail throughout the company. They will influence people coming into the company to be that kind of people. They will also help people within the company who experience setbacks and get "off the beam" to recover their optimism and enthusiasm so achievements can flourish again and rewards satisfy.

Concern for people needs to be at the heart of the company for the high standards to be credible to all the people involved in the company. If a company does not care about its people, they will not believe the company really cares about anything that counts. Sound business practices do not permit disregard for people, for no business can exist without people, and "little people" are important as well as influential people. Angela works continuously to insure that the company she is associated with has a heart for people. Her own example demonstrates her concern for people's lives and happiness as well as for the profits they represent for the company. She acts out of a conviction that people are the most important factor in the business equation, and the human dignity of all people must be cherished and guarded no matter how high or how low anyone may be within a company organization.

And all of this must be done within a context of integrity. Forthright honesty, uprightness in personal relations, and equity in the conduct of business are all vital to the heartbeat of a company if it is to establish excellent standards and maintain high principles. Such integrity is essential if a company is to enjoy confidence from its own people, from its customers, and from other businesses. A biblical adage is fitting to state Angela's conviction in this regard, "A good name is rather to be chosen than great riches" (Proverbs 22:1).

Passeport Boutique was organized with these four sound principles set into the very foundation of the company. So it was from the beginning of her involvement with it, a party-plan company which is the handles for Angela's dreams. She has the challenge she has long sought, a challenge which calls forth her best in creativity and effort. That challenge is to help build Passeport Boutique into a company which will fulfill her dreams and highest aspirations of profitability and human enhancement.

Summary

When Dorothy was swept by the cyclone into the "Land of Oz," she was told by the Munchkins that she must follow a yellow brick road to the Emerald City. There she would find the Wizard who could help her dreams come true by showing her the way to go home again. She searched and searched until she found the Emerald City and discovered the city and the wizard were all part of a land of make-believe. There her friends, the Scarecrow, the Tin Woodman, and the Cowardly Lion, learned that by believing in themselves their dreams could come true. And there Glinda the Good Witch told Dorothy that the silver shoes she had been wearing all along would take her home again to Kansas.

When Angela was a little Italian girl in Brooklyn, she dreamed of being Janie and acting out the make-believe of going to lands "over the rainbow." Through the experiences of life she learned, as Dorothy's friends in Oz learned, that brains and heart and courage are things you can have if only you will make yourself believe you have them and then act as though you have them.

Angela learned that there is no wizard who will make your dreams come true for you, for confidence in yourself is the wizard of your dreams. She found in party-plan sales the yellow brick road to success and wealth. She found in her own shoes the way to get to the land of her dreams.

And along the way every new venture for Angela was a new adventure, and every challenge was met with enthusiasm and determination. Her venture into Passeport Boutique ownership with her partners was a new challenge to new dreamed-of achievements for her. That challenge, like every challenge, was greeted by Angela with the same enthusiasm as in childhood she thrilled at the very idea of playing the part of Janie. Like an excited child, she still almost jumps from her chair to say, "I can do it! I can do it!"

Angela believes YOU can be the wizard who finds the answers to your dreams. She believes YOU can do it too — through party-plan selling!